50 DIGITAL TEAM-BUILDING GAMES

50 DIGITAL TEAM-BUILDING GAMES

FAST, FUN MEETING OPENERS, GROUP ACTIVITIES AND ADVENTURES USING SOCIAL MEDIA, SMART PHONES, GPS, TABLETS, AND MORE

JOHN CHEN, CEO OF GEOTEAMING

WILEY

JOHN WILEY & SONS, INC.

Published by John Wiley & Sons, Inc., Hoboken, New Jersey.
Published simultaneously in Canada.

For general information on our other products and services or for technical support, please contact our Customer Care Department within the United States at (800) 762-2974, outside the United States at (317) 572-3993 or fax (317) 572-4002.

Wiley publishes in a variety of print and electronic formats and by print-on-demand. Some material included with standard print versions of this book may not be included in e-books or in print-on-demand. If this book refers to media such as a CD or DVD that is not included in the version you purchased, you may download this material at http://booksupport.wiley.com. For more information about Wiley products, visit www.wiley.com.

Library of Congress Cataloging-in-Publication Data:

Chen, John, 1967-
    50 Digital Team-Building Games: Fast, Fun Meeting Openers, Group Activities and Adventures Using Social Media, Smart Phones, GPS, Tablets, and More / John Chen.
        Includes index.
    ISBN 978-1-118-18093-8 (pbk)
    ISBN 978-1-118-22737-4 (ebk)
    ISBN 978-1-118-24031-1 (ebk)
    ISBN 978-1-118-26502-4 (ebk)
        1. Teams in the workplace.   2. Social groups.   3. Information technology–Social aspects.   I. Title.   II. Title: 50 Digital Team-Building Games.
    HD66
    658.4′022—dc23

2012000944

Printed in the United States of America

10 9 8 7 6 5 4 3 2 1

CONTENTS

50 DIGITAL TEAM-BUILDING GAMES QUICK START

Use this Matrix to quickly find the digital team-building game that fits your needs.
Turn to the Preface and read "How to Use the Games in This Book."
Run your first digital team-building game and start to reap the rewards!

How to Use This Matrix

- First determine the goal of your team-building game by choosing one of the nine major categories.
- Next, narrow by the number of people you have, the time available, and the technology you have available.
- Then use the page numbers to scan the team-building games that match your goals and criteria and choose the one that fits your needs the best.

If you have any questions, you can ask at http://50digitalteambuildinggames.com. Thank you and happy digital team building!

Name	Page #	Web Browser	Tablet	Digital Camera	Video Conferencing	Web Conferencing	Presentation Software	Whiteboard	Teleconference	e-mail	Twitter	Chat	Smartphone	Text SMS Cell Phone	Participants	Time (minutes)	Closers	EPIC Team Building	Collaboration	Creativity and Innovation	Problem Solving	Improving Performance	Trust	Communication/Games for Speakers	Icebreaker
Me in 140 Characters or Less—Twitter Hypernetworking	9					X			X		X	X		X	2–1,000	10									X
Alpha Names—Learn Names While Learning Team Process	13					X			X			X		X	4–20	10–20									X
Where in the World Whiteboarding—Draw Who You Are and Where You're From	15							X		X					2–20	5–20									X
Photo Booth—iPad 2 or Photo-Based Networking	16		X							X	X	X		X	4–30	10–20									X
Pinterest—Pin Pictures and Websites for a Common Topic	20	X									X	X		X	2–1,000+	10–20									X
Texting Q&A—Ask Anonymous Questions Via Text	25										X	X		X	2–1,000	5–30								X	
Raising Hands—Have You Ever…?	27					X								X	2–1,000	5–10								X	
Polling—Team Consensus by Technology	29	X									X	X		X	2–1,000+	5–10								X	
TwitterStorm—Crowdsourcing Goodness	31								X		X	X		X	2–1,000	10–20								X	

(Continued)

xiii

	The Johari Window—Discover Team Blind Spots	Video Matching and Mirroring—Build Instant Team Rapport	Skype Interview—Capturing Team Knowledge through Video Interviews	A to Z—The A to Z of Building and Speeding Up Team Process	Grid Unlock—Collaborative Team Problem Solving with Shared Spreadsheets	Marshmallow Challenge—Build a Tower, Build a Team	Customized Jeopardy—Test Teams' Retention of Information	QR Scavenger Hunt—Scan Your Way to Team Building
Page #	57	60	62	67	68	70	73	76
Technologies								
Web Browser	X				X		X	
Tablet								
Digital Camera								
Video Conferencing		X	X			X		
Web Conferencing							X	
Presentation Software								
Whiteboard					X			
Teleconference								
e-mail								
Twitter								
Chat				X				
Smartphone								X
Text SMS Cell Phone				X				
Participants	1–15	4–12	2–1,000	4–12	4–12	4–1,000	4–40	2–1,000
Time (minutes)	10–30	5–30	5–30	5–30	15–30	45–60	10–30	30–120
Goals								
Closers								
EPIC Team Building								
Collaboration								
Creativity and Innovation								
Problem Solving								
Improving Performance				X	X	X	X	X
Trust	X	X	X					
Communication/Games for Speakers								
Icebreaker								

Page #	Name	Web Browser	Tablet	Digital Camera	Video Conferencing	Web Conferencing	Presentation Software	Whiteboard	Teleconference	e-mail	Twitter	Chat	Smartphone	Text SMS Cell Phone	Participants	Time (minutes)	Closers	EPIC Team Building	Collaboration	Creativity and Innovation	Problem Solving	Improving Performance	Trust	Communication/Games for Speakers	Icebreaker
83	Move One Line/Add One Line—Team Creativity with More Than One Solution	X													2–1,000	10–30					X				
91	Consensus Voting—Choosing Top Team Options Online	X						X							4–1,000	15–30					X				
95	Like to Move It—Quick Spatial Team Diagnosis	X													2–1,000	30–60					X				
98	Project Matrix—Balance Time, Quality, and Performance to Complete a Project	X													5–1,000	30–60					X				
100	Chat Survivor—Setting Team Priorities and Making Hard Decisions					X									2–1,000	30–60					X				
105	Twaiku—Twitter Poetry in Motion								X		X	X		X	1–1,000	10–20				X					
106	One Text at a Time Expert—Team Answers One Text at a Time	X									X	X		X	2–1,000	5–20				X					
108	WWMTD?—What Would My Team Do If They Had to Make a Creative License Plate?	X													2–1,000	10–30				X					

(Continued)

xv

Name	Page #	Web Browser	Tablet	Digital Camera	Video Conferencing	Web Conferencing	Presentation Software	Whiteboard	Teleconference	e-mail	Twitter	Chat	Smartphone	Text SMS Cell Phone	Participants	Time (minutes)	Closers	EPIC Team Building	Collaboration	Creativity and Innovation	Problem Solving	Improving Performance	Trust	Communication/Games for Speakers	Icebreaker
Team Pictionary—Communicating through Drawing	110	X						X							2–1,000	10–45				X					
Mind Mapping—Visual Brainstorming for Teams	114	X													2–1,000	10–60				X					
YouTeams—iMovie-Based Team Building	117		X												2–200	60–240				X					
GooseChase—Cell Phone Photo Scavenger Hunt	120												X		2–1,000	30–120				X					
Team GarageBand—Build a Song, Build a Team	121		X												2–1,000	60–120				X					
Office Move—Working Together to Switch Places	127	X													6–12	20–30			X						
Mergers and Reorgs—Getting Two Teams to Collaborate and Integrate Rapidly	130							X							8–10	20–30			X						
Broken Squares—Giving Is Better Than Getting for Team Collaboration	132	X													5–1,000	20–60			X						
Team Timely.is—Collaborating a Month's Worth of Tweets and Updates	135	X													2–90	10–30			X						

Table of technologies and goals for team-building activities (pages 136–165).

		Technologies															Goals								
Page #	Name	Web Browser	Tablet	Digital Camera	Video Conferencing	Web Conferencing	Presentation Software	Whiteboard	Teleconference	e-mail	Twitter	Chat	Smartphone	Text SMS Cell Phone	Participants	Time (minutes)	Closers	EPIC Team Building	Collaboration	Creativity and Innovation	Problem Solving	Improving Performance	Trust	Communication/Games for Speakers	Icebreaker
136	Team Haiku—Write a Team Haiku/One Word at a Time Online	X													2–1,000	10–20		X	X						
138	Team Case Study—Simultaneous Team Editing	X													2–50	60–120			X						
143	SCVNGR—GPS Treasure Hunt for Team Building and Cross-Team Collaboration	X											X		2–1,000	60–240+		X							
150	Geoteaming—GPS Treasure Hunt for Team Building and Cross-Team Collaboration			X									X		2–1,000	120–240+		X							
156	Flash Mobs—Organize Your Team in Time and Space	X		X							X				2–1,000	5–20+		X							
161	Shout-Outs—Acknowledging Teammates								X	X	X	X		X	2–1,000	10–20	X								
162	I Commit to...—Public Commitment to Change								X	X	X	X		X	2–1,000	10–20	X								
164	Just Three Words—Micro-Assessing Your Team								X	X	X	X		X	2–1,000	5–20	X								
165	Digital Slideshow—Picture Your Success					X			X	X				X	2–1,000	5–10	X								

xvii

PREFACE: HOW TO USE THE GAMES IN THIS BOOK

I like to tell clients that they're investing in my company for all the mistakes we'll *not* make because we've already made them in the past. You're buying this book to avoid all the mistakes we've already made. This chapter has a checklist for you to follow when planning any digital team-building game. Think about a PIPE when you first begin—something that you can use to guide your teammates to a successful outcome on the other side (if you don't get clogged along the way). PIPE stands for:

- **Purpose**—*Why* are you holding this team-building event? What clear goals do you have for it? What do you want the results to be?
- **Initiatives or Team-building games**—*Which games* best match your goals, number of people, time available, and technology available?
- **Preparation**—*How* can you best prepare yourself and your teammates so that the team-building activity gives you the greatest odds of success?
- **Event**—*How* can you execute the best team-building event and achieve your team goals?

Purpose

Asking yourself the preceding questions is the most important step in using this book. I often ask people what their purpose is—especially for team building—and they often don't have an answer for me. Many times they give vague responses such as, "Build my team," "Communicate better," "Have less conflict," "Understand one another better," or "Have fun." Although these are all valid goals, today's business climate makes it critical to look at return on investment for the time and resources. When used effectively, team building can help teams do countless things better: complete a process in a shorter amount of time, unleash creativity to unearth a solution that wasn't previously possible, create positive relationships that help in the future, and generate resolutions that improve customer service and save resources (including cash). Successful team building uses small team-building games to mirror what's going on in the larger workplace situation. This approach allows groups to examine their behavior, find new ways of working, and apply it to their professional settings. I find that the greatest areas of improvement in all of my work come from team process and cross-team collaboration. The greatest gains a team can make are in their interactions with one another. Likewise, the greatest gains you can make in multiple team situations are interactions between teams.

Some examples of great team-building goals range from "Decrease team process time by 20 percent" to "Increase revenue by 15 percent" to "Increase customer satisfaction survey scores by 3 points." Other teams seek to "learn facilitation and leadership skills to promote new leaders" and "increase relationships between teams in disparate locations to increase collaboration after team building." Your goals may be just to have fun, blow off steam, increase morale, or reward employees for good performance. The most important thing is to keep the goal you've selected in mind and adjust your expectations accordingly.

If you're having a hard time forming your team goal, consider asking yourself these key questions:

- What is the current state of my team?
- What key result do I want out of this team? What result would justify the time to plan and take people offline for this amount of time?
- What would have to change to make that result easier?

Here's an example of how one particular company transformed a team-building activity into a competitive edge. A Fortune 500 company manager started his team-building event's purpose with the simple goal to "get people together." We discovered by asking deeper questions that 300 people from three different divisions were coming from Washington State; Fargo, North Dakota; and Copenhagen for the first time. They had just completed a product cycle, and because they came from different, recently acquired companies, this was the first cycle that would tightly integrate these different products into a single, seamless system. The goal was therefore to associate team members from different companies who fulfilled similar functions. In addition, revenue wasn't the measure for this business unit; rather, it was number of seats or licenses sold. All of these factors took the purpose for this event from a simple team building into a customized gathering that mixed employees from all three locations with each team of about eight people. It also encouraged the teams to collaborate with one another to achieve a company goal: to ship the next version of the product with tight integration. This team went on to record results including 21 percent growth and revenue in excess of $1.7 billion. This example highlights the powerful result that can occur when you discover and state the true purpose of a team-building event—and get the most out of bringing all of these people together in one place.

Initiatives or Team-Building Games

Once you've determined the purpose for your team-building event, you can then use this book to select the team-building games you need to make it a success. There is an easy-to-use chart in the Quick Start that can help you quickly find a team-building game that fits your purpose, the type of technology available to you, the number of people who will be participating, and the time you have available. For example, let's say that you need a quick icebreaker that builds relationships for 25 people in about 15 minutes over chat or Twitter. You can refer to the chart for all team-building games that match these requirements, one of which would be "Me in 140 Characters."

If you are using two or more team-building games, then it's also important to think about sequence. A good approach is to order the team-building games to make it easier to achieve the goals you've identified one step at a time. For instance, if one of your objectives is to achieve harmony in a group, then you should sequence the team-building games from the easiest to the most challenging, attempting to get the group to build up their skills along the way. You may want another, more overconfident group to understand how to overcome frustration in preparation for a bigger assignment. In this case, putting the hardest challenge first and getting them to realize that not everything is easy will allow you to complete deeper work by the end of the session. If the goal is building relationships, I'll often start with an activity that is twos (two people working with each other directly), then fours (teams of four working with each other), eights (teams of eight working with each other), and finally, an all-team initiative. This gradual process gives your team members the chance to get to know others in their group one initiative at a time and to feel gradually more confident as more people are added.

The following is a sample list of things around which you can sequence:

Time—shorter to longer

Technology—easier to harder

Difficulty—simple to complex

# of People—fewer to more

Relationships—fewer to more, shallow to deeper

Skills—beginner to advanced

Be sure to allow sufficient time for virtual or online training. You want to design your team-building event to keep energy high and have as many people be fully present as possible without burning them out. Shorter training sessions are usually better in this regard. It's also a good idea to give participants a break every 60 minutes or so if the team-building event is going to go longer than 1 hour.

Preparation

Test Your Technology

Technology definitely follows Murphy's Law: If it can go wrong, it will. Although technology can allow amazing things to happen, it can fail just at the time you need it most. To increase your odds of a successful team-building event, test your technology ahead of time. Did you know that, according to President Wayne Turmel of greatwebmeetings.com, more than 80 percent of first-time webinar presenters use their webinar for the first time *during* their webinar? In other words, even *professional presenters* don't know to test their technology. Get your own account, log in, and have one or two other people or computers to test each feature that you plan to use during the event. Be sure you know how to find and use key features prior to your event. Anticipate questions that participants may ask about the tools you are using, and see if you can have the answers ready.

Another good idea is to encourage people to log in or call in 30 minutes prior to the team-building event. This allows you time to resolve any last-minute challenges and start the event on time. A good tip is to list this extra half hour as informal social time; let people know that they can use it to catch up with one another while they are waiting for others to log in.

Prepare Your Teammates

Be sure to send out an e-mail or meeting request that lists the event's date and time, purpose, agenda, and technical instructions as early as possible. Then resend it or set reminders for 1 week prior to the even and the day of the event. If you use Outlook, a great tip is to use the Options > Delay Delivery option.

Right after you send your team-building event e-mail, you can send two more with the dates set 1 week before the event and the morning of the event. Just check the "Do not deliver before:" option and set the date and time to send.

Perhaps the most critical thing to do is to have your participants send a test message or install and use the technology before the event. Make sure you allocate time and resources for providing a help desk for those new to the technology. Keep track of each person who lets you know that he or she has connected successfully. Be proactive and set a date to call any team members who didn't report back—either because they were too busy or because they encountered an unforeseen problem. This step is crucial to ensuring that each person can participate fully during the team-building event. You don't want any kind of exclusion to occur, including technical exclusion, and that will be the case if a participant doesn't have the same capability as others. This can create a sense of distrust in those team members if you don't address the issue beforehand.

Participant Map

Another facilitator skill is to adopt the use of a participant map. Since you usually can't see all of your participants, the participant map is a way to visualize the people participating in your team-building event and keep track of their level of participation. We've included a template for a participant map (see Appendix or http://geoteaming.com/uploads/partici pantmap.pdf), and the concept is fairly simple. Just write each participant's name on the left-hand side. Next to that, leave space to write notes about that person—where that person is from, his or her job title, and maybe a personal fact that you learned about that person from one of the icebreakers. Finally, make a tally mark any time that person volunteers to talk during the team-building event at a specific time, and jot down a short note if that person makes a significant contribution. You'll get the sense as this map develops whether a group of people or a particular person is dominating the conversation. This will give you a way to ask someone for his or her impressions if that person hasn't said anything yet. Your teammates will appreciate the sense of inclusion you create by helping make sure everyone hears the unheard voices. You'll also ensure that everyone has the chance to say what he or she thinks, even if individuals choose to pass on commenting. Practice this with live meetings to get a sense of how it works; you may notice some unique patterns in your meetings.

Facilitator Tree

After you choose your team-building games, sketch out or type up a facilitator tree—a way to map out the different predicted ways that a team-building event can go. For instance, let's say that you have three team-building games and the team fails the first. How can you frame that letdown to help them achieve their goals instead of losing them over poor morale? Or perhaps the first initiative unearths potential deep challenges within this group. When building this map, I also assign "odds" to the scenarios I have. When I know enough about the team, I can predict and design what will usually happen during a team-building event based upon my experience and also plan for potential scenarios that could happen (see Figure P.1).

How can you be flexible with your timing to allow the real conversation to occur and uncover a key breakthrough in team trust that may be critical to your team-building purpose? Building this tree allows you as the facilitator to build the confidence to handle anything that might come up during the event. If you facilitate multiple sessions like this, your team will eventually teach you by presenting you with a situation you've never imagined. The facilitator tree will prompt you to create new solutions and capture the lessons you've learned.

During a team-building event for a large energy company, I had not planned for when a senior team member said, "It's Your Fault!" that his team and his company failed in today's event. On the fly I was able to present that the same scenario had been presented to over 950 companies and 50,000 people in the exact same way and turned his attack into a deep question of "Who is responsible for the result in this room?" The company finally concluded

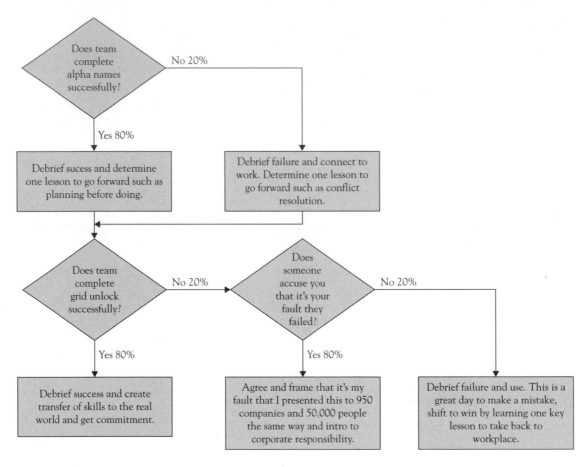

P.1 Facilitator Map

that they were responsible for the result in the room and it became a powerful lesson in personal and corporate responsibility. In addition, I now add the "It's Your Fault" branch to every team-building event so I'm prepared!

Plan B (C, D, and E)

Finally, because of the ever-changing pace of technology, it's valuable to make sure you have a Plan B (and maybe C, D, and E!) in the event that some of your technology does not work on the day of your event. Technology can fail at multiple points, many of which are not in your control, so make sure you have alternatives and more reliable options during your training.

I often choose two or more channels of communication in the case that one fails. A teleconference line is usually a very reliable and fault-tolerant form of communication. Despite some spotty cell areas, phone lines and teleconference bridges are highly reliable. Even if an individual's line fails, that person can just call right back in and join in where he or she left off without bringing the entire conference call down for the entire event. For instance, it would be very useful if I were doing a Twitter-based team-building event to have a teleconference connection to greet people, give clear instructions, and get feedback before and after the event. You can also complete many of these team-building games in a live setting with everyone in the same room. This is a great way to see future virtual connections, make people comfortable participating through technology if it's new for them, and then give everybody a live channel to ask real-time questions, connect a face to a voice or online ID, and gain valuable insights in the debrief. For speakers, trainers, and presenters, using digital team building is a new way to engage your live audience using new technology.

During your planning, one strategy could be to use the most reliable technology for Plan A, then desirable features or new technology for Plan B, a highly reliable but less desired or older technology as a Plan C, and analog cards and pens for Plan D when all else fails.

Event

Now that you've done all the hard work, you're ready to complete the PIPE with an actual event.

Log in Early

Have everything you need ready; make sure you used the restroom; have a glass of water nearby; reboot your computer the morning of the meeting so you know it's fully operational and has the least amount of software running; and then log in up to 30 minutes early to make sure all of your technology is working correctly. Just as you would arrive to give a speech an hour early, arriving online is just as important and gives you time to meet your guests after you make sure everything is working correctly.

Create Invitation and Inclusion

Imagine that your first guest is coming to a party where he or she doesn't know anybody—because logging in online often feels just like that. As soon as you hear the tone that tells you that someone arrived, find out who it is and greet him or her. Ask the attendee something about himself or herself and continue the conversation until someone else calls in. As each person arrives, ask for his or her name and acknowledge that person's presence. I also write each person's name down so I know who is in the "room" (see Participant Map or http://geoteaming.com/uploads/participantmap.pdf). I'll read off all the names of the people who are present when I'm ready to begin so that everyone knows who is on the call. I then check to see if I missed anyone who called in. Once everyone is accounted for, I begin the meeting.

Improv and Engage

Now that you've done all the planning for a great event, remain open to the possibility of your ever-changing audience's needs. The participants want you to succeed and gain the value of the training, so discover their interests, add humor, and personalize the event for them. Many of the best training moments occur when the audience begins to take over and engage in a deep conversation that doesn't require the facilitator; this is often a sign of successful training. Using the participant map allows me to keep track of when participants talk and helps me notice when someone hasn't said anything for a while. When this happens, you can call on the more reserved people to see if they have anything they'd like to add. This attempt to include them shows that you're paying attention as the facilitator and making sure that everyone is engaged and not checked out (or involved in other activities like reading e-mail; you'll be amazed at how attentive team members will become when they are called out by a facilitator and it's clear they are not engaged).

Facilitate Success

No matter what happens—if your team members fall short horribly or if all your technology fails—look to facilitate success in any way possible. You've thought ahead about the many ways this event could go, so you should be ready to facilitate positive learning out of any potential event. I believe—and share with others—that, "Today's a great day to make a mistake." Quite often, there's not as much at stake in a team-building game, except a little ego, pride, and maybe a small prize. I always say that if your participants can learn the lesson here, they can then use it to avoid some very expensive mistakes at work. A great paralegal once told me, "We play games so we can make better decisions in life." Find any way to facilitate success, and your audience will thank you in the end.

End on a High Note and Follow Up

Be sure to use some type of reflection and closure to your event that ends it on a high note. From hearing the team's new commitments from the closer "I commit" to watching your team on the closer digital slideshow to recounting the great stories that took place during the event, you must find a way to end on a high note. Ending on a high note is the last thing every participant will remember and increases the odds that they will be motivated to make a change back at work or at least look positively on the time they invested.

Make sure to follow up as soon as possible on anything you promised after everyone logs off. Whether it's sending the chat log, a link to photos, or a link to resources, send or post them as soon as possible—before you get caught up with something else. You can relax once you've completed all your obligations, knowing that you put on an amazing team-building event.

Facilitator Debrief

The final step is take a few minutes to reflect and write down your and your team's pluses and deltas. *Pluses* are the things that went great during this training, whereas *deltas* are potential areas of improvement—ways to make this training even better the next time you do it. This simple practice will make each training session better, and after 100 trainings, all your incremental improvements will make you a seasoned expert. Award-winning customer service trainer Pete Winemiller says, "It's not doing one thing 100 percent better that makes a difference, it is doing 100 things one percent better."

Digital Team-Building Games Checklist—PIPE

- Purpose
  - Why are you doing this team-building event?
  - What results do you want for your team?
  - Make sure everything you do helps move you toward your goal.
- Initiatives or Team-building games
  - Which team-building games best match your goals?
  - How many people will be participating?
  - How much time is available?
  - What technology is available?
  - How am I sequencing my team-building games toward my final goal?
- Preparation
  - How can I best prepare myself and my teammates before the team building starts to give me the greatest odds of success?
  - Has all the technology to be used been tested?
  - What is the most reliable technology you have?
  - What will you do if your technology fails?
- Event
  - Log in early.
  - Create invitation and inclusion.
  - Improv and engage.
  - Facilitate success.
  - End on a high note and follow up.
  - Debrief.

ACKNOWLEDGMENTS

A decade ago, my advisor, Dr. Simon Priest, and I dreamed of a day that we could facilitate team-building events online with people from around the world. We dreamed of creating a "digital ropes course." We tested the ideas and got amazing results with initial audiences, such as increasing trust between two people by more than 20 percent with a short 30-minute video conference. A team at Boeing generated more than 150 e-mails in just 20 minutes as part of an experiment in accelerated ways of learning how to work with one another. Dr. Priest and I formed a company called Virtual Teamworks (virtualteamworks.com), but like many great ideas, it was simply before its time. Thirteen years later, the American Society for Training and Development (http://astd.org) declared 2010 the year of social media as a viable training vehicle. The year 2011 was named the year of mobile learning, or mLearning.

How Twitter Made This Book Happen

I have presented team-building sessions at the ASTD national conference for many years, and in 2011, I proposed a brand new session called TweetTeams: Twitter-based team building. I used a Twitter-based tool called HootSuite to promote the session throughout the conference. I opened a *free* 1-hour consulting session to get anyone on Twitter prior to the presentation, and I brought four new iPad 2's to let people borrow during my session so they could create all new content.

What happened is team-building magic that can happen only with technology. I recruited two volunteers to help with Twitter consulting, Lauren DiSalvo and Kelly Titus, both of whom I met in prior years on Twitter and at the ASTD tweetup (a tweetup is a meeting organized through Twitter). During this TweetTeams session, I personally helped a woman from South Africa who had never tweeted before send out 20 tweets before the end of the session (training at its finest). More than 120 people attended this session, and many remarked that I opened new ideas on how they could use social media for team building at their work. And then Richard Narramore from John Wiley & Sons, Inc., approached me and asked me if I wanted to write a book on digital team-building games. Wow! This was a one-in-a-million opportunity—and now it's happened.

I tell you this story to impress upon you that technology can literally change your life. Although it may be scary at first, learning the new tools to communicate and build trust will bring your team-building skills to a new level. The team-building designs in this book are both really cool *and* effective. For example, if you have the technology, you can engage in team building at any time, from anywhere in the world, without the expense and time to travel. In addition, you can engage in digital team-building events live to inspire more online interaction when you're not face to face. You can open or close meetings with these initiatives. Best of all, when properly executed, your group can reap the rewards of increased communication, trust, and results.

I want to thank my amazing kids, Max, KJ, and Kelson, who keep me up to date on all the latest digital trends and allow me to Facebook their life; you are amazing gifts in my life and blow me away with the games you play in life. Thank you to many of my original team-building mentors, including Dr. Simon Priest, who was influential during the early years of Geoteaming and worked side by side to apply Simon's extensive experience; all the facilitators from the Association for Experiential Education (aee.org) who set the foundation; and my coach, Matt Beucler, who helped me start it all, teaching me many of my facilitation skills and helping me make the big jump from Microsoft. A huge shout-out to my Geoteaming team, including Jo Ann Fjellman, Jackie McGlauflin, Michele Keele, Tanya Phillips, Bill Angel, Carissa Zenorini, Jack W. Peters, Mick Pearson, Peter Gaylord, Donna Lowe, and so many more geotechs who have worked with us. Thank you to my reviewers, Holly Duckworth, Anne Chen, Ruth Knipe, Jackie McGlauflin, Michele Keele, Debbie Reddy, Bryan Roth and May Leong, who tested every team-building game in this book. It truly takes a team to produce every book and I appreciate each and every one of you!

Thank you to Holly Duckworth who gave the ultimate gift when I was writing this book; your heart, spirit, passion, and support mean the world to me. And most of all, thank you to Richard Narramore and the team at John Wiley & Sons, Inc., for believing in me, making this book happen, and helping me complete a cherished goal on my lifetime bucket list!

INTRODUCTION TO *50 DIGITAL TEAM-BUILDING GAMES*

Why Should You Buy This Book?

Are you a trainer or presenter who has to use more and more technology? Are you a manager who needs to build a team that lives in different time zones and can't always bring your team together face to face? Are you a team leader who is looking for ways to build teams of a younger, tech-savvy generation? Then this book is for you. Even if you're a technophobe, have never tweeted, or have never posted an update on Facebook, this book is here to show you that the key elements of communication and trust are at the heart of every team-building event and that all this crazy new technology just provides a different way to communicate and trust. Once you begin to make meaningful connections over existing technology such as Twitter or Facebook or whatever is popular now, or prompt them to use new technology in fun ways, you're ready to reap the benefits of one of the most precious commodities: your teammates' attention and time.

The digital team-building games in this book will help you reap the intangible rewards of being cool and current, but they will also help you improve morale, build relationships, and develop a high-performing team that creates greater results with fewer resources, under budget, and on time!

Technology is a great magnifier. It can magnify good and bad teamwork very quickly. This book will help you harness good teamwork and magnify it with technology, allowing you to do things that were impossible 20 years, 10 years, and even 1 year ago.

Where the Games Come From

I've been involved in using technology for team building for more than 25 years. For more than 14 years I've owned my own company, Geoteaming, which uses GPS and other technology to create team-building adventures that lead to better group performance. In 14 years, my team and I have worked with more than 950 companies and 50,000 participants, creating innovative games and simulations with technology. During that time, we were named the Meeting Professional International's (mpiweb.org) Supplier of the Year, were named in the Top 25 Fastest Growing Minority Company list three years in a row, and were the Better Business Bureau's Innovative Business Practices Winner; I was named a Top 40 Entrepreneur Under the Age of 40 and *Training* magazine's (trainingmag.com) Top Young Trainer.

More important, we've made stronger teams from small companies with five people to Fortune 500 companies like Microsoft and US Bancorp. We've led events for the Entrepreneurs' Organization that included as many as 700 people and events for DECA with up to 1,750 attendees. In one interesting project, we worked with REI, the world's largest co-op. Their flagship store was operating five different stores under one roof. To meet an aggressive sales goal, the store manager knew that the five main departments needed to work better together. After an amazing all-day team-building event where this team became one of

3

the seven highest-scoring teams we've worked with, they went on to collaborate and exceed their aggressive sales goal even in a recession. What game do you want to play and win?

The Education of a Digital Team Builder

I learned my "team building with technology skills" at Microsoft, where I worked for a decade helping to manage and ship more than 10 products in 10 years, including Microsoft Exchange, the first client/server-based e-mail system. Exchange took more than eight years to develop and had five successive general managers before Brian Valentine stepped in and closed the deal. Exchange consisted of eight different parts that were bought, acquired, or developed internally. The first time we put them all together, if you sent e-mail to 10 people, the server crashed and didn't return control to you for 24 hours! Needless to say, we had a slight performance problem.

Brian hand selected 14 leaders for the project including me. He brought the leaders into a room and said, "We have a performance problem. It's your job to fix it." Then in classic Microsoft style, he left the room. We were all looking at one another wondering what to do; then we all jumped in. I did the first thing I knew how to do in a situation with multiple teams: I *blamed* the other teams! It must be their fault for being so slow. But careful analysis showed me each component was fast, for what it was designed for.

When the initial blaming ended, we mapped out the entire communication between all the teams through the client and the server and brought leaders from each of the eight components to review the map. I confessed that I'll never be smart enough to know or fix any of your components; all I know is this is what is happening, that it takes 43 round trips to the server to read *one* e-mail and it's all of our jobs to fix it. I sat down and endured the longest two minutes of silence as each team leader read through the list. Then like alchemy, the room erupted in good ideas for improving cooperation and efficiency between the eight different components of Exchange.

If there's anything I've learned over the decades that I've done team building, it's this: the greatest gains a team can make is in the communication between team members and the communication between teams. Eventually, to improve communication among software development teams at Microsoft, I created a game, a game involving doing the most with the least amount of resources. Over the course of the next 2½ years, we expanded our performance tests to more than 50 major scenarios. We took software scenarios like opening an e-mail and took it down to a theoretical minimum of 0 resources. We got crafty and did our research; we knew that more than 50 percent of the time, when you read one e-mail, you also read the next e-mail. Our solution was to program Exchange to read both e-mails at the same time in one round-trip to the server.

This led to some extraordinary results. We were able to simulate more than 10,000 users on a server, we earned two US patents for the unique work we had done, and the product has sold more than 100 million client licenses in its lifetime. This is a huge cash cow for

Microsoft, and it was amazing to be a leader who helped build an incredible team culture that produced results.

What's interesting is that out of the 950 team-building events I helped to lead at Geoteaming, only seven teams, less than 1 percent, have ever achieved the highest score possible. Why is that? It turns out that the majority of people have no idea how to get multiple teams to collaborate. And that's where the biggest performance payoff is. My goal in this book is to share with you the secrets of how to build a high-performing team, how to create clever cross-team collaboration, and how to accelerate the process with technology. Despite diversity, attitudes, distance, cultures, gender, and any other obstacles you may have, I want to show you how you can leverage technology to build teams that defy the odds and create not incremental results, but revolutionary results!

This book has quick, simple, and proven games that your teams will enjoy, that will make them work together better, and that will make you look good, even if you're not already comfortable with technology. With this book you can achieve this—without too much preparation—and you can find a fun way to get your team comfortable with critical new technologies that can lead to business breakthroughs.

If you experience these results, I invite you to share your story with me by e-mailing john@geoteaming.com or via my blog, blog.geoteaming.com. If you run into problems with a game, I'd love to know your ideas on how to make it even better for you in your world. I look forward to meeting you online and in the analog world and hearing *your* stories of team success. It is my heart's desire to distill more than 20 years of passion for team building and technology and teach you at least one thing that helps you increase the strength of your team.

What is digital team building? It's a fun new approach to team building that will keep you and your team current. It can liven up a meeting or presentation. It can nudge people into using new technology and skills. It can build team relationships and skills. Building on key research from Dr. Simon Priest (summarized at http://geoteaming.com/uploads/georesearch.pdf), digital team building speeds up teamwork processes by 40 percent. In other words, when you buy this book, you can do more with less and produce breakthrough results.

Icebreakers

Icebreakers are great openers for most team-building events. They introduce people, help them find out each other's names, and kick off the team-bonding process. These are especially important when new teams are forming. You can also use them anytime you add a teammate or want to discover something new about your team, even if the team members have worked together before. You can put these kinds of initiatives together very quickly and easily, and they help put the group at ease. You can also use icebreakers when you're introducing a new piece of technology. Make sure to start with the most basic of functions when using a new piece of technology for an icebreaker.

Me in 140 Characters or Less—Twitter Hypernetworking

Time: 10 minutes

Participants: 2–1,000

Technology: Twitter, text, chat, teleconference, web conferencing

Category: Icebreaker

Goals

Get to know about each team member and assess needs.

Game Summary

This icebreaker solves simple challenges such as knowing everybody's name, associating at least one word with that person, finding things in common, and beginning to understand the other person's personality and style. It's also a great opening initiative for people who are new to Twitter. Once you've logged on to the Twitter website, this initiative trains your teammates in how to use it, keep their posts short, use features to find out information about other team members, and most important, learn the names and something about each teammate.

Setup

Arrange a time and unique hashtag to meet at (such as #50dteambuilding) if you are using Twitter. Using chat, send instructions on how to set up a Twitter account and how to search messages or view only messages using your unique hashtag. Note that you can go faster if you also have a teleconference line set up.

Instructions to the Audience

Since we're a new team, let's find out who is on this team and a little bit about each other. Go to twitter.com and log in with your username and password. Now let's search for only the messages we want to see by typing "#50dteambuilding" into the Search box at the top and hit Return.

Since Twitter has a 140-character limit, you'll have to keep it short and sweet. Click the "New Tweet" box with the pencil in it near the top right ⌨️.

Tweet the hashtag (i.e., #50dteambuilding), where you are from, what you do, and something unique about yourself in 140 characters or less.

For example, my tweet would look like this:

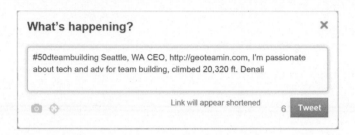

Any questions?

Okay, you have 5 minutes to complete your tweet and read other people's tweets. Remember to refresh Twitter (by hitting F5 on most Windows Internet browsers, Command+R for Mac users, or clicking the "Reload current page" button ↻) to read other people's introductions. Also, you can click their Twitter ID to find their full name and information about them.

Power Tips

Learn how to attach photos, videos, or links to other sites as a way to say much more than 140 characters of narrative.

Click on each person's Twitter profile to see a picture of that person and his or her short bio. Read the bio and click the link to that person's website. This will provide you with a lot of information about this person.

You can send a link to your participants in the meeting request that will take them to your hashtag search, https://twitter.com/#!/search?q=%2350dteambuilding (replace "50dteam-building" with your hashtag).

Debrief

What did you learn about one another? What do you notice that you had in common with others? What challenges did you have in describing yourself in 140 characters or less? Whom do you feel closer to after completing this? Why? Do you know each other's names now?

Variations

Feel free to customize the last question to gain information that you want to know about each teammate. For example, you could ask, "What do you want out of this team-building course?" as a way of doing needs analysis.

Case Study

At a monthly gathering of our Washington State Chapter of MPI (mpiwsc.org), we met technology expert James Spellos. For this event, everybody's name tags included printed instructions to tweet their name, company, position, and favorite app or technology during the 30-minute networking period before lunch was served. About 40 people, out of 100, tweeted their information. During the 5-minute time reserved for structured networking, the MC then read the different tweets as each person stood or waved as they were read. This allowed the participants to get to know 40 of the people there. In addition, we received feedback on what apps people are using and which ones they like. The following is the Twitter log from this event:

bigkid #mpiwsc Welcome to August MPIWSC Meeting of Hot Technology with James Spellos http://t.co/lUxkK3z #mpi #eventprofs

bigkid #mpiwsc We will be running a high tech networking today. Tweet your name, company, position and your favorite app or technology #eventprofs

bigkid #mpiwsc John Chen, Geoteaming http://t.co/w2qLPGN, CEO, http://tweetdeck.com is one of my fav apps.

briannajmark Brianna Mark, Seattle's CVB, Special Projects Manager, fav app is seesmic (for now). #Mpiwsc

bigkid #mpiwsc Chris Dunham, Meydenbauer Center, convention sales, fav app is Shazam in car, last song was from radio!

jspellos #mpiwsc - My fave app today is Spotify. What a game changer for music lovers!

bigkid #mpiwsc Terry Onustack, IASP, Meetings Manager, www.IASP-pain.org, I heart Facebook.com

bigkid #mpiwsc Jane Schmidt, LaConner Channel Lodge, director of sales, posting town specials, daily deals, spa deals at Facebook.com

bigkid #mpiwsc Sarah Nelson, LaConner Channel Lodge, dir of sales, groupon.com, sold 500 nights in 8 hours!!!

bigkid #mpiwsc Adrienne Miller, Suncadia, Natl sales manager, blackberry for e-mail!

briannajmark Chad Biesman, man of leisure, undercover tourist Disney world app #mpiwsc

bigkid #mpiwsc Carrie Zimmerman, renaissance Seattle, SR sales manager, Facebook.com and conference apps for Cascadia briannajmark Roxy Inouye, biz admin, Msft, Netflix for windows phone #mpiwsc

nashfung Nash Fung - professional magician And basketball frenetic! Fav. App=photo-synth at #mpiwsc

SeaJet01 #MPIWSC Jeannette Davidson, Gretchens Shoebox Express, sales mgr, facebook

bigkid #mpiwsc Angela shen @savorseattle savor Seattle food tours founder, TiVo dvr fav show top chef

bigkid #mpiwsc jeff Kyle, mra services, it director, spiceworks, network monitoring and it community

TerrenceYoung My fav app is HootSuite whats yours? #mpiwsc

bigkid #mpiwsc Jason Henderson, mra services, registration manager, my android tmobile g2, always on it

bigkid #mpiwsc Karen Davies, meeting planner, founder, google translate used in Finland on my last trip

thebekah #mpiwsc Bekah Laughman, Sheraton Bellevue Hotel, Business Travel Sales Manager, Fav App: Instagram ;o)

SBDonaghy #MPIWSC Everett Blindheim, SH Worldwide, web/reg team, iPhone

Azureeyes30 #MPIWSC, Amy Adams, Suquamish Clearwater Casino Resort, Sales Manager, Words Free

Witt_emily #mpiwsc Emily Witt, Hyatt Regency Bellevue, Catering Sales Manager, C25K app

lyevan #mpiwsc, Lesley Young Cutler, president, Envision Meetings & Incentives. My smartphone!

kathygerke #MPIWSC Kathy Gerke, CRG Events, Account Manager, Bejeweled

AlkiGirl09 #MPIWSC, Carolyn Henning, Director of Catering. Fav App - Facebook

emilgoo #MPIWSC, Emily Gooding, Starwood Hotels and Resorts, Account Director Starwood Convention Collection, fav app? . . . . app envy

SingingComedian #mpiwsc Larry g jones entertaining you at up to 75 voices per hour. From Sinatra to Cher, to rodney dangerfield I get no respect at all

beck_seattle #MPIWSC, Becky Williams, Director of Catering, McCormick & Schmick's, great app is Flashcards, helped in studying for CMP

michaeljnoesen #mpiwsc my fav app is Starbucks mobile card.

SBDonaghy #MPIWSC SarahBeth Donaghy, SH Worldwide, Registration & Events Mgr, LinkedIn to connect w/ my clients & kicking butt at Wordsfree for fun!

audreyrfan #mpiwsc Audrey Fan. eVenues.com (new startup). Angry birds

HRHalsey #mpiwsc Heather Halsey, microsoftmeeting solutions customer advocate. I love Facebook.

MPIWSC RT @thebekah: @MPIWSC Bekah Laughman, Sheraton Bellevue Business Travel Sales Manager, Fav App: Instagram #mpiwsc

MPIWSC RT @jspellos: @MPIWSC looking forward to today's Technologies session #mpi #eventprofs. cool video to show. #mpiwsc

bigkid #mpiwsc James Spellos uses tweetchat.com

briannajmark Revised fav app is angry birds. #Mpiwsc

SBDonaghy Everything @jspellos is saying abt social media & technology for today's meetings is so spot on! #MPIWSC

TerrenceYoung Are u using paper.li or delicious or scoop.it or other daily RT if u do! #MPIWSC #mpi #eventprofs

jones_kristen Kristen stevenson, visit bellevue washington, convention sales manager, my favorite app is Pandora! #mpiwsc

SBDonaghy @jspellos . . . I love the #winepad! #MPIWSC

SeaJet01 Check in with foursquare! #Mpiwsc

bigkid #mpiwsc mad props to James Spellos for all his tips, note less than 5% use some of these features, should it be you? #eventprofs @jspellos

bigkid #mpiwsc chapter breaks 300 for facebook friends! http://t.co/262bTUz Like them today to get to 400! #eventprofs #gmic #pcma #somet

Alpha Names—Learn Names While Learning Team Process

Time: 10–20 minutes

Participants: 4–20

Technology: Text, chat, needs to be real time (not Twitter as it has a significant delay), teleconference (optional)

Category: Icebreaker

Goals

Text or chat all of your names in alphabetical order.

Game Summary

This text or chat initiative looks deceptively simple; however, it can become challenging without a leader. It's also an easy way to learn everybody's name and something about their team style in a short amount of time. Using this initiative, a facilitator can learn the team's default style and process.

Setup

You can use the chat feature on any instant messenger, BuddyMeeting.com, or other meeting room. The key is to use a real-time chat application. Do *not* use Twitter; each reader has a different refresh rate, which makes it difficult to use for these types of timing games. It's also useful to have a stopwatch ready to time how long the team takes.

Instructions to the Audience

We're going to get a chance to meet one another and see how fast we can work as a team. Chat all of your first names in alphabetical order. If you get one out of order, you need to start again from the beginning, and you can use only chat to communicate. Any questions?

Power Tip

The fastest technique I've seen is to have your name pretyped in and know the order in which the team needs to go in, hitting Enter as soon as you see the name before you.

Debrief

Who was the leader in the group? How did you decide on a process? What did you do when you failed? How can you do it even faster?

Variations

Allow the teams to complete the game two or three times in an attempt to increase their speed with each try. It can make the game too easy if their names are displayed on the app they're using, so you can have them chat A-Z in alphabetical order instead.

Case Study

We did this activity with one especially dysfunctional team of 10 people. They asked no questions before they started, spent no time on process, and just started working using trial and error. Joe would type his name, then Beth would type hers, and they'd have to start over. They would get three or four names done, and then someone would go out of order. They'd get to five or six, and someone would chime in with a suggestion; although often helpful, it meant starting over yet again.

This team realized during the debriefing that a clear team leader would have helped them, even though nobody wanted to fulfill that role. They also realized that using their planning time would have allowed them to ask more questions, agree on the plan they were going to use, and then execute it. This provided a significant comparison to how they were working as an online team. They were doing redundant work at multiple sites and not taking the time to plan who was doing what before starting a project.

Implementing these changes in future team meetings yielded significant gains in productivity and opened more time and energy for team training to create further gains!

Where in the World Whiteboarding—Draw Who You Are and Where You're From

Time: 5–20 minutes
Participants: 2–20
Technology: Whiteboard
Category: Icebreaker

Goals

Write your name and draw something to represent where you are from.

Game Summary

It usually takes attendees a good amount of time to arrive for online meetings. As such, this initiative is a great way for a facilitator to engage people one by one as they log in to the meeting. Each person who arrives is able to see information about the other people who are present and then join in themselves.

Setup

Log in to any whiteboard or online conferencing software such as BuddyMeeting.com, GoToMeeting, or another Web conferencing tool with a whiteboard. As the facilitator, be sure to log in 15 minutes before the start time and draw your own example. Use the service's teleconference line or have a call-in line.

Instructions to the Audience

Welcome! Who just joined us? (Wait for responses from attendees.) Thank you for coming; we're all taking a moment to introduce ourselves. I'm passing control to you, so please write your name and a quick sketch of where you're calling from on the whiteboard.

Variations

You can ask participants what their favorite hobbies or type of weather is, what company they work for, and other questions that might spur graphic art.

Case Study[1]

During the online meeting that produced the preceding graphic, we had John from Seattle (that's the Space Needle), Fred from St. Louis (the Arch), Jane from Hawaii (a surfer on a wave), Vanna from New York, and Liz from Skagit Valley, Washington, where a tulip festival is held. As each person finished their drawing, other participants chimed in with comments; they chatted about the last time they were in Hawaii and asked where Vanna lived in New York, thereby spurring some helpful informal conversations that allowed everyone present to get to know the other participants.

Photo Booth—iPad 2 or Photo-Based Networking

Time: 10–20 minutes

Participants: 4–30

[1]*Sources:* Priest, S. #4 of *100 of the Best Virtual Team-Building Events.* (Seattle, WA: Tarrak Technologies, 2001). virtualteamworks.com; http://www.tarrak.com/BOOKS/100.htm

Priest, S., Sikes, S. & Evans, F. #37 of *99 of the best Experiential Corporate Games We Know.* (Lakebay, WA: eXperientia, 2000). http://www.tarrak.com/BOOKS/99.htm

Technology: iPad2 (live), Twitter, e-mail, text, or any other tool that can send a photo
Category: Icebreaker

Goals

Take a photo of yourself and share with the group.

Game Summary

The iPad 2 features an app called Photo Booth that allows you to take a photo of yourself using one of nine different filters, including Squeeze, Kaleidoscope, and Thermal Camera. This is a good introduction to the forward-facing camera on the iPad 2, and it can easily break the ice, as you can make some very funny photos with it. Other options are to have people use their own camera phones to take their photos and have them text or e-mail the photos with a caption. You can exhibit all of them by displaying pictures on a projector from a computer or using a program that can share your desktop, such as BuddyMeeting.

Setup

Have at least one iPad 2 that you can use or check to see if enough participants have cell phones with cameras and the capability to text or e-mail a photo. Another option is to make digital cameras available that you can collect and from which you can quickly download photos.

Instructions to the Audience

Pass the iPad 2 around and take a photo of yourself using one of the nine different filters available. Then be ready to introduce yourself as we display your photo.

Variations

Consider using the Magic Mirror app on the iPad 2; this uses augmented reality to allow the user to try different virtual hairstyles, glasses, and other accessories. The app follows the user's face, keeping the virtual accessories in the correct place. You can touch the "camera" icon to save the photo to your Gallery and then e-mail or tweet it from there.

Case Study

We brought an iPad 2 into a meeting with Expedia as a way to display new technology-based team building. Each person in the room took his or her photo, added it to iMovie (see YouTeams), and wrote a caption before passing it to the next person. Here are a few of the photos they took, along with the captions they came up with:

Too much caffeine

Ah ha...fun at team building equals fun at work.

We have X-ray eyes

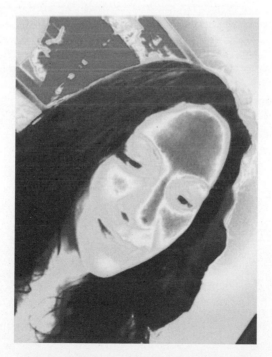

TEAM . . . together everyone accomplishes more!

Pinterest—Pin Pictures and Websites for a Common Topic

Time: 10–20 minutes
Participants: 2–1,000+
Technology: Web browser
Category: Icebreaker

Goals

Find out what your team has in common in regard to a specific chosen topic by pinning websites and photos to Pinterest.

Game Summary

Pinterest is a cool website that allows you and others to pin a website or a photo to a visual board. It's a great networking activity, because you can discuss the different links people share and use them to discover what you have in common with one another. In addition, you can keep the board up for future networking.

Setup

You (and possibly all of your teammates) need to sign up for a free account at Pinterest.com. You can then create a board with the topic and invite your teammates to contribute.

Instructions to the Audience

Let's find out something about each other by logging into the website Pinterest.com and posting at least one or more links or photos that fit our topic. I'll give you 5 minutes to post as many as possible; then we'll see what we have for our team.

Sample Questions

Where do you want to travel? What are your favorite websites? Can you share some photos of your family/friends?

Debrief

Take the time to review the board and ask each person to introduce himself or herself and describe at least one pin. At the end, ask what you learned about this team through the various links people shared.

Case Study

Julie Norton from one of our Fortune 500 clients started a board after her husband surprised her with a trip to France. She asked people to share their "Places to go," and others soon began pinning up their favorite destinations. This site has the most beautiful collection of photos from around the world and great ideas for places to visit. Julie currently has 46,000 people following this board, with more joining every day. Now that's power icebreaking!

Source: http://pinterest.com/julie_m_norton/places-to-go/

2

Communication/ Games for Speakers

I t takes a lot of communication to build a team. Ironically, the best team communication happens when a team communicates without saying a word. The team member knows where to be, when to be there, and what to do—and that happens only with practice, practice, practice.

The collection of games that follows focuses on team communication: how members interact with one another and how they communicate with you as the presenter, speaker, or leader. The skills that these exercises help build range from texting to digitally raising a hand to learning better teleconference protocol when presenting online. Many of these games are designed to help speakers persuade an audience of any size to interact with you, the leader, thus making your presentation more interactive and engaging. Communication and trust are the foundation of teamwork, and these games are best used in the early stages of team development, often as the second initiative after an icebreaker.

Texting Q&A—Asking Anonymous Questions Via Text

Time: 5–30 minutes

Participants: 2–1,000

Technology: Cell phone text, Twitter, chat

Category: Communication

Goals

Get reluctant or shy people to participate.

Game Summary

Ask and answer challenging questions by submitting them anonymously. This interactive audience participation allows many people to submit questions to a speaker at the same time and is a great way to compel people to bring forth various issues. It creates participation with the group, and members feel a connection when the speaker addresses their questions. Although this activity works best in person, you can also use it online via teleconferences and webinars.

Because texting as a mode of general communication has become so popular, Texting Q&A has also become hugely popular, especially with members of Gen X and younger groups. In addition, the anonymous aspect allows participants to ask difficult questions that they may be reluctant to ask using a microphone—that is, if they had to speak the words. Another benefit is that you can avoid dead mic time at the end of the presentation by telling people they can send a question at any time during the presentation.

Setup

Choose a cell phone that you can use during the presentation, and include its number on your PowerPoint or presentation slides. You can either opt to display it on every slide (by adding it to the master slide) or you can reserve it for a single slide at the start of the presentation. Next, decide which questions you'll ask and choose an MC to read through them. It's best not to take on this role yourself, as you may have dead time while the audience waits for you to read the questions and choose one. Although you can say the questions will be anonymous, know that you are receiving the phone number of the person on the other side and it is up to you to respect their privacy and identity; a good practice is to delete all the texts after your presentation if you want to maintain their anonymity.

Instructions to the Audience

I will take questions throughout this entire presentation. Feel free to text *any* questions to this number, and I will answer them at the end. Since it's anonymous, you can truly feel free to bring up *anything* that's on your mind! Those viewing online can text questions in on their cell phone, too.

Power Tips

You can video the answer to these questions and post them on a YouTube or other video hosting website to continue to get value from Texting Q&A. If you are answering the questions by Twitter or a chat room, you can save the text from the answers and turn it into a blog post or written article for those who could not attend the session to read.

Debrief

While just answering the Texting Q&A questions can be enough, you can delve deeper into the process and ask debriefing questions of what it was like to use Texting Q&A versus using a microphone for live questions. You can use questions such as:

Did you like using Texting Q&A versus a microphone or asking questions live?

Did you ask deeper and more challenging questions because it was anonymous?

Case Study

Mars Hill Church, which has locations all over the country, made texting Q&A famous when they started integrating it into their sermons. Participants began asking questions that ranged from the philosophical ("Can God judge me?") to the curious ("What about sleeping at a Christian girlfriend's house but not having sex?") to the controversial ("Is aborting a pregnancy from a rape wrong?") This example makes clear how this approach has the potential to elicit authentic questions and promote a deeper sense of learning than you might encounter when using a microphone. It's also an effective way to create trust with executive team presenters, because it conveys the fact that this team is ready to be open and tackle an organization's difficult challenges.

You also have the opportunity to expand this approach beyond the original event, which Mars Hill Church did by recording the answers to the questions their parishioners asked.[1] They created a YouTube channel[2] to address these, which has more than 9 million views at last count.

Raising Hands—Have You Ever . . .?

Time: 5–10 minutes

Participants: 2–1,000

Technology: Web conferencing

Category: Communication

Goals

Test and increase audience listening and engagement while gaining quick survey results.

Game Summary

Ask each participant—or instruct your participants to ask one another—a series of questions and gather their responses via digital hand-raising.

GoToMeeting used this very simple interactive initiative during a webinar, and it turned out to be one of the session's biggest hits. The group liked it because it easily encouraged audience participation in a short amount of time, provided instant feedback, and allowed participants to become facilitators by giving them the chance to influence the questions being asked. This initiative makes it easy to ask questions such as "Have you ever . . .?" to discover what members of the team have in common.

---

[1]http://blog.marshill.com/2008/05/06/live-texting-at-mhc/
[2]http://www.youtube.com/watch?v=r-kTO0mTAyM

Setup

Start a Web conference using BuddyMeeting.com, GoToMeeting, or another Web conferencing tool with virtual hand-raising capability. Find the Status column on the left-hand side in the Users window; this will show you how many people are raising their hands. If you are using another web conference tool, make sure you take the time to survey the features and see if it has a hand-raising tool. You can test this capability by clicking the ✋ icon on the bottom right. As the presenter, you can clear hands by clicking on the user's hand icon in the Status column. Finally, be sure to set up a teleconference so that you can give instructions by phone.

Instructions to the Audience

(These instructions were based on using buddymeeting.com. Please make sure to modify these instructions for your web conferencing tool before sending out.) Let's find out what this group has in common and what the members want to know about one another. First, please find and click the Raise Hand icon in your Users window. (Wait for responses.) Good; now please lower your hands by clicking it again. (You can click on any hands to lower them if the users can't do it in time.) I'll ask the first question and if you can answer "yes," click the Raise Hand icon. When I ask you, lower your hand and then I'll ask another question. If you'd like to suggest a question, type your question in the chat window on the right side of your screen. Okay, the first question is . . .

Power Tips

GoToMeeting has a dashboard that gives you the total number of people raising their hands and what percentage this is of the total group. They also have a Lower All Hands feature that allows you to start over again quickly for your next question.

Debrief

What did you find that you have in common with this team? What question did you find the most interesting? What answer surprised you the most? Do you feel like an insider or an outsider to this team? What strengths do you think this team has? What weaknesses or challenges do you think this team has?

Variations

Good first questions include "Can you hear me?" "Have you ever attended a webinar before this one?" "Have you ever managed one or more people virtually?" "Have you ever traveled internationally?" "Have you ever owned a smartphone?" "Have you ever led a webinar and not prepared for it?" "Have you ever sent an e-mail you wish you didn't?" and "Have you ever posted a status update online that you wish you didn't?"

You could choose all the questions, or have participants send chat messages with their questions or pass control to the next person and have each person ask a question they want to know about each person in the group.

Case Study[3]

HR.com used Raising Hands at their Virtual Conference on Social Media on November 3, 2011. The following link contains a list of the questions that were asked, the majority of which were generated by the people attending the teleconference.

You can view this recorded example of Raising Hands at the following link, starting at the 33:00 mark: http://www.hr.com/en/webcasts_events/webcasts/archived_webcasts_and_pod casts/digital-team-building_gthoq0dm.html.

Polling—Team Consensus by Technology

Time: 5–10 minutes

Participants: 2–1,000+

---

[3]*Sources:* Priest, S. & Rohnke, K. #7 of *101 of the Best Corporate Team-Building Activities*, 2nd ed. (Tacoma, WA: Tarrak Technologies, 2000). http://www.tarrak.com/BOOKS/101.htm

Priest, S., Sikes, S. & Evans, F. #35 of *99 of the Best Experiential Corporate Games We Know*. (Lakebay, WA: eXperientia, 2000). http://www.tarrak.com/BOOKS/99.htm

Technology: Cell phone text, polling websites, Twitter, polling widget that can be used with PowerPoint or other presentation tools.

Category: Communication

Goals

Poll your team on a multiple choice, open-ended question or goal poll and display the results instantly on the Web or using PowerPoint, Keynote, or another live display.

Game Summary

PollEverywhere.com allows you to create a poll for 30 people for free, and other polling sites, such as TwtPoll and MightyQuiz.com, also handle polling. SurveyMonkey is another way to conduct a poll via e-mail. It's a great way to get feedback from a lot of team members in a short amount of time, and you can then use the responses to find trends in your team.

Setup

Poll Everywhere has an impressive 30-second setup for a free poll that will allow up to 30 responses: http://www.polleverywhere.com/login. Type in your e-mail and a password and click Sign In. Just type in your multiple choice or open-ended question, and it creates a website that displays the results.

Instructions to the Audience

Let's see what the team thinks about these current issues. We're going to take a couple of quick polls and find out where we are.

Power Tips

Facebook has a built-in polling feature called "Ask Question" (📊 **Ask Question**); it's located as the third option at the top of the log in area. Click Ask Question, enter a question into the edit box, click "Add Poll Options" at the bottom left of the edit box, and add the choices you'd like for this poll. Click Post and your poll is live. In addition, you can click "Ask Friends" and send direct invites to anyone on your friend list to send them a message to answer your poll.

Case Study

As one of Cascadia's team of volunteers, I worked with other individuals to produce the 2010 Meeting Professionals International (MPI) Cascadia Educational Conference (mpicascadia .com), a collaboration between the Washington and Oregon chapters of MPI. Validar (validar.com) sponsored a text-polling system for our event. We used this system at the end of every educational session to gain immediate feedback on our speakers and the overall conference, and we gave it to the speakers at the end of every day to let them know how they did. In addition, we pioneered the first postconference debrief with organizers, trade show participants, and sponsors to inform them of how effective the conference and their participation were a mere 30 minutes after the conference ended. We were able to gather feedback on what participants thought was great and what they thought could be even better. Our overall poll showed us that 91 percent of the participants learned something that they'll use at work—information we used to help promote the following year's attendance.

As a team—and especially as volunteers—we felt great pride in what we created and were thrilled to provide a tangible result back to our community. It significantly boosted team morale and allowed us to more easily recruit and build teams for the following year's conference—97 percent of whom claimed that they learned something at the 2011 Cascadia Educational Conference that they would indeed use to produce results in the workplace.

I learned something at Cascadia that I will use at work to produce a result. [*Pick One*]
Of 47 total responses, there are 44 responses to this question. (93.6%)

	Prompt	Count	%
A	Agree	40	(90.9%)
B	Neutral	4	(9.1%)
C	Disagree	0	(0%)

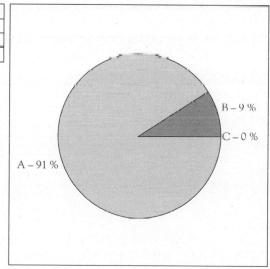

Source: MPI Cascadia Educational Conference (http://mpicascadia.com) Polling Results.

TwitterStorm—Crowdsourcing Goodness

Time: 10–20 minutes
Participants: 2–1,000
Technology: Twitter, text, chat, teleconference (optional)
Category: Communication

Goals

Increase communication between presenter and participants. Tap the power of your entire audience to brainstorm and share new resources, solutions to a problem, or ideas on how to make a process faster or better in a short amount of time.

Game Summary

This simple Twitter, text, or chat initiative gives the power of parallel. Every single person can contribute in the same, brief time period, and you can easily gather more than 100 new ideas or resources. In addition, conducting this exercise at conferences produces a huge amount of activity from your session that can add value to other participants who are watching the Twitter feed both locally and remotely.

Setup

Create a unique hashtag on Twitter or use an existing hashtag such as a conference hashtag (e.g., #astd12); add the hashtag to your slides with the question or topic that you're arranging. You can also use free online tools such as HootSuite Archives (http://help .hootsuite.com/entries/20757068-how-to-create-an-archive) or The Archivist (http://archi vist.visitmix.com/) for archiving all of your results to share with your audience after the presentation.

Instructions to the Audience

We're going to tap the power of the audience by participating in a massive brainstorming activity called a TwitterStorm. I'm going to set a 4-minute timer and play one song, during which time you can answer this question.

Sample Questions

What is the best technology that you use? What's a tangible business result that social media has brought to you? What's the best team you've ever been on—and what made it so great? What is a solution to [insert your customized problem here]? What do you want to get out of this session?

Power Tips

Use HootSuite Archives to save an archive of all the responses. Then, you can publish or send it to your meeting's attendees to share all the ideas for the future.

If people are sharing devices and are tweeting under one username, have them add their names to the tweet so that you can give them credit as you go through the ideas.

Debrief

Take the time to read through the results and recognize the people who contributed. This allows you to find out who is in the audience and match an online name to an actual person, thereby strengthening your connection with other team members or the audience.

Case Study

Currently, more than 500 public Twitter chats take place weekly. As moderators look for new formats, TwitterStorm can be a great initiative to add value to these chats.

On September 29, 2011, I moderated a Twitter chat for #eventprof (Event Professionals) and did a TwitterStorm of the best tips and tools for using Twitter. Just 28 tweets provided us with resources to more than 64 different Twitter tools, including Klout.com, a site that measures an individual's level of online influence.

1. *Twitter Search*—Is, obviously, Twitter's own search function. You can subscribe to a search via RSS.
2. *TweetBeep*—Is like a Google Alerts for Twitter.
3. *Tweet Scan*—Allows you to schedule Twitter searches to be sent to your e-mail.
4. *Twist*—Is like Google Trends for Twitter.
5. *Twitscoop*—Is a real-time tag cloud of Twitter buzz that also allows you to create graphs based on keyword tracking.
6. *MicroBlogBuzz*—Tracks the most popular links shared on microblogging services, including Twitter, Jaiku, and Identica.
7. *Twit(url)y*—Tracks popular links and displays them in Digg-like fashion.
8. *Hashtags.org*—Tracks the most popular Twitter posts that include a hashtag. You can subscribe to an individual hashtag using RSS.
9. *Twemes*—Tracks Twitter memes.
10. *TweetGrid*—Creates a Twitter search dashboard that updates in real time.
11. *Monitter*—Is a real-time keyword-based monitoring service that lets you watch three columns of keyword streams side by side. You can subscribe to them using RSS.
12. *Retweetist*—Tracks the most popular retweets.
13. *minn.citytweets.net*—Shows real-time tweets from and/or about Minneapolis.
14. *Qwitter*—Notifies you when someone unfollows you in Twitter.

15. *Spy*—Tracks real-time keyword mentions in Twitter, FriendFeed, Flickr, Blog Comments, Yahoo! News, blogs, and Google Reader and allows you to subscribe via RSS.

16. *TweetWheel*—Finds out which of your Twitter friends know each other.

17. *Twitter Charts*—Gives you a visualization of when a particular Twitter user is most active. This is an excellent tool to determine the most opportune time to engage a given person.

18. *twinfluence*—Ranks Twitter users' influence.

19. *Twitter Grader*—Grades a given Twitter user according to influence. Includes power users by geographic location; suggests who to follow and allows you to check if someone is following you.

20. *TwitterSheep*—Creates a tag cloud of all the words in the bios of a given Twitter user's followers.

21. *Twitter Counter*—Provides stats on a given Twitter user and lets you compare that user to two others.

22. *Twellow*—Is a Twitter directory.

23. *Tweetboard*—compares Twitter users side by side.

24. *TweetStats*—Gives you Twitter statistics about a given user.

25. *TwitterMeter*—Allows you to enter a word to graph its use on Twitter's public feed.

26. *TwitterLocal*—Is a desktop app that finds Twitter users within a fixed radius of a city or zip code.

27. *Twitter Analyzer*—Offers a ton of Twitter statistics. The best Twitter analytics tool I have found to date.

28. *MrTweet*—Is a recommendation engine that also provides statistics on your Twitter usage.

29. *Localtweeps*—Finds tweeps near you.

30. *Twits Like Me*—Suggests Twitterers who are like you.

31. *Retail Twitter Aggregator*—Aggregates the Twitter feeds of a handful of bricks-and-mortar retailers.

32. *retweetradar*—Tags clouds and trends of retweets.

33. *Twubs*—Finds hashtags.

34. *What the Trend?*—Finds hashtags that are rising in popularity.

35. *Tagalus*—Is a hashtag dictionary.

36. *Twitclicks*—Shortens URLs and tracks clicks.

37. *Bit.ly*—Shortens URLs, counts clicks, shows who else shortened a URL, and provides metadata about that URL from across the Web.

38. *Tweetburner*—Shortens URLs and tracks clicks on Twitter and FriendFeed.

39. *Twittervision*—Shows real-time geographic posts to Twitter.

40. *TweetChannel*—Creates Twitter channels.

41. Twitterfall—Monitors Twitter in real time.

42. *Twendz*—Is a real-time Twitter search engine coupled with related keywords and word clouds.

43. *Tweetzi*—Is an advanced Twitter search engine.

44. *Twistory*—Pumps your Twitter feed into a calendar application so that you can visualize your tweeting history.

45. *TwitLinks*—Tracks the most popular tech links from the most popular tech twitterers.

46. *Twitturls*—Tracks popular links.

47. *OneRiot*—Is a Twitter search engine.

48. *twopopular*—Tracks hashtags and keywords in real time or by time intervals.

49. *TweetVolume*—See how often words and phrases are mentioned on Twitter.

50. *TweetEffect*—Find out which tweets resulted in you gaining followers and which tweets caused you to lose followers.

51. *TweetMeme*—Tracks the most popular links on Twitter every 5 minutes, categorized by types of content: blogs, images, video, or audio.

52. *Tinker*—Aggregates Twitter conversations around topics.

53. *Splitweet*—Is a multiaccount manager and brand monitor.

54. *Tweetizen*—Lets you categorize your followers and then follow only that feed.

55. *Who Should I Follow?*—Finds new Twitter friends.

56. *FriendOrFollow.com*—Finds Twitterers you follow who don't follow you back.

57. *TwitterFriends*—Compares your tweeting behavior with others'.

58. *Who Follows Whom?*—Allows you to select up to five Twitter users to see who they follow and who follows them in common.

59. From Howard Greenstein at *Social Media Today*:

    a. *Tweetvisor*—Is a Twitter control panel.

    b. *TweetDeck*—Is an Adobe Air desktop application for Twitter. I actually use this. It should've been on the original list.

    c. *PeopleBrowsr*—Is a dashboard for many social media accounts, including Facebook, Flickr, OpenID, Digg, FriendFeed, and, of course, Twitter.

    d. *CoTweet*—Lets multiple people manage a single Twitter account in a rational fashion.

    e. *TweetLater*—Lets you schedule tweets and vet followers.

60. *Klout*—Measures your social media effectiveness.
61. http://t.co/TZmlXCg2—Includes the article "How to Become the #1 Tweeter at Any Conference."
62. *HootSuite*—Allows you to tweet to five different places at once, time them, and get analytics.
63. *BedJump*—Is a good example of a unique niche group.
64. *TwitHawk*—Find real-time conversations talking about your topic and location.

The following figure is the actual log from TwitterStorm:

date	time	username	status
9/29/2011	9:40 AM	bigkid	RT @wilhelmus: @bigkid It means you'll be checking every day wondering y your score is going up or down for no reason ;) #eventprofs
9/29/2011	9:39 AM	bigkid	@justinlocke #eventprofs Klout in 140 char or less http://t.co/5Jv7Aiej From 1-100 your ability for true reach, amplification and your net
9/29/2011	9:39 AM	entBuy	@corinnekessel Did u register? @justinlocke Use tab on left 2 find influencers & style. Klout measures social media influence #eventprofs
9/29/2011	9:37 AM	justinlocke	b4 i invest time, may i ask, what is klout, in 140 characters or less? #eventprofs
9/29/2011	9:37 AM	bigkid	#eventprofs My @Klout score is 42. I improved it by 3 points over the past day! http://t.co/s2i5IxCp - What does this mean??
9/29/2011	9:36 AM	Pogby	Great resource! RT @entBuy: Heres a great list of other tools to measure the influence of your tweets: http://ow.ly/6IDxN #eventprofs
9/29/2011	9:36 AM	CorinneKessel	@bigkid @entBuy @klout I just did mine. I am 45. now what? #eventprofs
9/29/2011	9:36 AM	entBuy	All UR time is wasted trying 2Tweeting if U don't have ways 2 measure the influence of your content. What else do #eventprofs use to track?
9/29/2011	9:35 AM	bigkid	#eventprofs We had @wilhelmus talk at our PCMA/MPI Summit and he gave hilarious link bedjump.com as example of niche online community!
9/29/2011	9:35 AM	CorinneKessel	According to @Klout, @CorinneKessel's Klout score is 45. How influential are you? http://t.co/EuM1leSh #eventprofs
9/29/2011	9:35 AM	justinlocke	@entBuy it depends on what you;re selling. big diff between a commodity item/svc and a big ticket item like a speaker. #eventprofs
9/29/2011	9:34 AM	entBuy	Here's a great list of other tools to measure the influence of your tweets: http://ow.ly/6IDxN #eventprofs

(continued)

(*continued*)

date	time	username	status
9/29/2011	9:33 AM	bigkid	#eventprofs @jspellos gave me this new link, http://t.co/NRzPAFtC for Twitter marketing...
9/29/2011	9:32 AM	entBuy	@bigkid http://t.co/KVQ0Ldwj #eventprofs It's an AMAZING tool for anyone that's serious about #social media
9/29/2011	9:32 AM	justinlocke	@entBuy my articles do some, but mostly it is stil plain old pre-internet word of mouth. #eventprofs
9/29/2011	9:31 AM	bigkid	@entBuy #eventprofs I don't measure @klout but I probably should, how do I do that?
9/29/2011	9:30 AM	entBuy	@justinlocke What have you found your customers relate to best if not Twitter? FB? email marketing? #eventprofs
9/29/2011	9:30 AM	bigkid	#eventprofs I think another easily overlooked feature in TweetDeck and other is click on profiles, info appears in right hand column
9/29/2011	9:29 AM	entBuy	Do you guys measure your @Klout? That's also helpful to measure your top influencers. #eventprofs
9/29/2011	9:29 AM	justinlocke	@bigkid twtr use is not yet established in a lot of my customer bases. #eventprofs
9/29/2011	9:27 AM	bigkid	#eventprofs @entBuy I also use HootSuite to schedule a series of tweets into the future, I did that for #astd breakout and got 120 in room!
9/29/2011	9:26 AM	TahiraCreates	RT @bigkid: #eventprofs Here's my 10 tips on how to be #1 tweeter at any conference. http://t.co/TZmlXCg2 I was #1 at 2010 WEC (not easy!)
9/29/2011	9:26 AM	justinlocke	@bigkid well lessee, besides #eventprofs, there's #speakchat, #engage365, #sobcon. lot of overlap, feels like the club.
9/29/2011	9:26 AM	bigkid	#eventprofs I also like the Twitter app for iPad because it integrates a lot of links (to web, pics and more)
9/29/2011	9:25 AM	entBuy	A1 Well all this clutter talk has def. brought upfeeds & platforms. I've heard TweetChat & Hootsuite today. What else do #eventprofs use! #1
9/29/2011	9:24 AM	bigkid	#eventprofs Here's my 10 tips on how to be #1 tweeter at any conference. http://t.co/TZmlXCg2 I was #1 at 2010 WEC (not easy!)
9/29/2011	9:22 AM	bigkid	#eventprofs OK, let's share cool Twitter tips or tools, what your favorite app, tool or technique on Twitter?

Twitter Tools to Track Tweets:

(updated in 2009 and still valid) http://ow.ly/6IDxN

A Good Overall How-To Guide for Twitter Chats:

http://socialfresh.com/twitter-chat-how-to/

Current List of More than 500 Twitter Chats Happening Weekly:

https://docs.google.com/spreadsheet/ccc?key=0AhisaMy5TGiwcnVhejNHWnZlT3NvWF
VPT3Q4NkIzQVE&hl=en#gid=143

Go Ahead, Caller—Improving Teleconference Skills with a Game Show

http://www.mikogo.com/wp-content/uploads/2010/01/teleconference.jpg

Time: 10–30 minutes
Participants: 2–20
Technology: Teleconference
Category: Communication

Goals

Learn how to improve teleconference skills and results by playing a game show.

Game Summary

Teleconferences are still a reliable way for teams to meet and do productive work. Because it
is a proven technology, there are a lot of great resources, such as FreeConferenceCall.com,

that provide teleconferences for free. This initiative teaches teleconference processes that participants can use for future calls, while also learning about teleconference etiquette or other trivia topics for which you can provide a variety of questions.

Setup

Arrange a teleconference using a provider such as FreeConferenceCall.com. For instance, we use 218-844-3366 and choose a unique PIN number, such as #434343. Send an e-mail or otherwise communicate to all other teammates the date and time that they need to call in. Have the instructions and questions ready to read before the meeting time and call in at least 10 minutes before the start time to make sure the line is working and to greet teammates as they "arrive."

Instructions to the Audience

Today we're going to learn a new teleconference process that will help the efficiency of our telecons—and we're going to do it by playing a game called Go Ahead Caller. Think of it like a radio call-in game; I will read a question and you will "buzz" in by saying your name, for example, "This is John." I will acknowledge you by saying, "Go ahead, John," and then you can take a shot at answering the question. You get a point if you answer correctly, and someone else will get a chance to answer if you're wrong. Let's test the buzzers one at a time by starting with Jane. Jane, go ahead and "buzz" in by saying, "This is Jane." (She does so.) "Go ahead, Jane. Next?" (Proceed to test and check for everyone on the line so that you can hear them.)

Okay, let's start Go Ahead Caller:

True or False?

(As discussed, after each question, wait for a participant to answer. The correct answers are given here after the true/false statement.)

You should always wait until the last person calls in to begin the meeting. — FALSE

You should learn to use the Mute button at the correct times. — TRUE

You should call from an open office space or other loud environment. — FALSE

You should shuffle papers and sit in a leather chair during the call. — FALSE

You should end the conference on time or early. — TRUE

You should write down all the names of the participants on the call. — TRUE

You should mute your call, especially if there is hold music. — FALSE

You should turn on all your ringers for phones, pagers, and computers. — FALSE

You should use negative confirmation such as "Is there anyone who does *not* have the handout?" to make sure the team agrees. — TRUE

You should call in 5 minutes early. — TRUE

Power Tips

Remember that one benefit of teleconferences is that the entire conversation doesn't stop just because one caller has technical challenges. That person can simply call back in and rejoin the conference with minimal disturbance to the group.

As the facilitator for this call, *continue* to use this protocol and correct anyone who is not doing so by using gentle reminders, such as "Who is this talking?" and guidance such as "I'm going to let Jane talk, and then I'll get back to you, Fred."

Variations

Occasionally, I plan a segment called CrossTalk, during which two or more teams can talk to each other to solve a current challenge or set up another time to talk if it the topic requires more attention.

I also create a participant map (see Appendix) for teleconferences. I type or write each person's name (it depends on how loud my keyboard is; writing can be a quieter alternative) with a timeline at the top, and then I make a mark or note each time someone talks during the call. This helps me identify people who haven't said anything; I can call on or direct comments to the more reserved members if I realize that a particular person is dominating the conversation.

Case Study

I developed this teleconference style while working at Boeing on a project called Transition to Management I. It was an amazing class in that the video produced told parallel stories. You could click on each video to see more of what was happening behind the scenes of the various management situations. The company also held weekly audio teleconferences as the situation was revealed.

During the teleconference—which had about 12 people on it—I noticed (by using a participant map) that one individual, an Asian woman, had not said anything for the first 40 minutes. When I asked her what she thought of the situation, she was able to provide a completely different point of view from her peers. She actually predicted the next revealed scenario—something we hadn't sent to her yet. This information would not have been available without her contribution and it turned the team's decision making in a much more productive direction after her revelation.

Model Citizen—Testing Communication Assumptions by Building a Model They Can't See

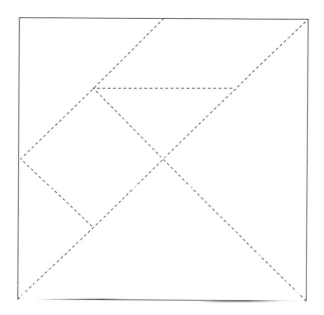

Time: 30–60 minutes

Participants: 2–1,000; teams of 4–8

Technology: e-mail, text, chat, Twitter, teleconference

Category: Communication

Goals

Discover communication channel assumptions using a technology where members can't see the other team.

Game Summary

This is a great initiative to test teams' assumptions in situations where they can't see one another. Groups will develop skills and ask questions about what the team has on "the other side," something that will lead to reduced process mistakes in the future.

Setup

Arrange a teleconference, e-mail, text, Twitter, or chat for a specific date and time for all team members to gather at. Go to a tangram website, such as http://www.amblesideprimary. com/ambleweb/mentalmaths/tangram.html, that allows you to move and rotate the tangram shapes and create a completed model. You can also find completed tangram model shapes on the Internet by searching. Take a screen shot of the completed tangram model and send it to one team. Send the link to the tangram website to the other team. Make sure that all teams with virtual tangrams know how to take a screen shot (or teach them how to do so: PrtSc on a Windows computer; Command+Shift+4 on a Mac). Then have them send it to all other team participants and the facilitator (you can do this via a "Reply all" e-mail, a text, or a tweet of a photo in Twitter).

You must establish which teams will be Model Teams and which will be Builder Teams, and with whom they will be paired. Either use the breakout feature over teleconference or make sure the Builder Team has the Model Team's telephone number so that they can hang up from the conference and call one another. Set up e-mail between teams and copy the facilitator so that he or she can see and evaluate all communication between them. If you're using Twitter, you can set up hashtags such as #team1, #team2; the facilitator can search on #team to see all messages between the teams.

Instructions to the Audience

Today you are going to learn about the assumptions teams tend to make when using certain communication channels. You and your teammates are going to become Model Citizens: the Model Teams will have a completed model, and the Builder Teams will use virtual tangrams to build the model. Builder Teams, does anyone *not* have your virtual tangrams? (Help send the link to any builder teams.) Model Teams, does anyone *not* have the completed model? (Send the completed model to any Model team who does not have it.) Okay, Builder Teams, you will have 15 minutes to complete building the shape that your Model Team has. You cannot use any visual communication until I tell you so. Any questions? Go!

(Wait 15 minutes.)

Now that the time is up, please take a screen shot of your screen (see Appendix on how to take a screen shot) and send it to the facilitator.

Power Tips

You can send the color version of this tangram; and you can re-color the virtual tangram with different colors than the original. This will be an additional challenge as one team will ask about an orange triangle and the other team will not know that it is a different size orange triangle and can be addressed in the debrief on how virtual teams make assumptions on what the other team sees on the other side.

Debrief

You can ask questions before and after the teams reveal their pictures: What was easy about working with your other team? What was challenging? What assumptions did you discover? How did you discover them? On a scale of 1 to 10, how confident are you that you built the correct model? What did you learn from this? What will you do differently in the future when working with a virtual team?

Variations

You can give the teams unlimited time if you want them to have higher odds of success, or you can change the different models to fit a theme of your meeting.

Case Study[4]

This game was a favorite of one of my managers at Microsoft who went on to be the general manager for the Microsoft Dynamics division. He originally conducted this initiative live. The Microsoft manager realized that he got stuck in referring to a triangle by a certain color; although another person had a triangle of the same color, it was a different size than the one in the model. Both failed the task and ended up becoming pretty frustrated. This had a huge impact on this individual's communication style as a manager; he still remembers the lesson today and keeps in mind how vital it is to *not* make assumptions when working with his teammates and to ask questions about his assumptions before he believes them to be true. He's now the manager of more than 1,400 people in a division with more than $1 billion in revenue! We replicated this same game at Boeing with six managers via e-mail. As a result, we generated 150 e-mails in about 20 minutes in which we tracked different teams' progress at varying times and found similar lessons in communication assumptions over e-mail that were very difficult to interpret on the other side. This ultimately led to a failure to build the model correctly, a lesson that paid dividends in their jobs, where they work with remote teams to assemble aircraft.

Tangram Websites

Free tangram model: http://www.creativeimaginations.net/PAGE7.HTML

Color tangram: http://www.juegotangram.com.ar/tipostangram/VariantesImagFull/fletcher .jpg

Tangram solution: http://www.dimensionsguide.com/wp-content/uploads/2010/05/ Tangrams-Dimensions.png

Virtual tangrams: http://pbskids.org/cyberchase/games/area/tangram.html and http://www .amblesideprimary.com/ambleweb/mentalmaths/tangram.html

Backchannel—Instant Feedback by Group Text

Time: 5–60 minutes

Participants: 2–1,000

Technology: group texting app, such as GroupMe, Facebook Messenger, or Fast Society on a cell phone

Category: Communication

---

[4]*Sources:* Priest, S. #80 *of 100 of the Best Virtual Team-Building Events.* (Seattle, WA: Tarrak Technologies, 2001). virtualteamworks.com; http://www.tarrak.com/BOOKS/100.htm

Priest, S., Sikes, S. & Evans, F. #35 *of 99 of the Best Experiential Corporate Games We Know.* (Lakebay, WA: eXperientia, 2000). http://www.tarrak.com/BOOKS/99.htm

Goals

Create a channel of instant feedback for a team that allows the team members to communicate with one another during a presentation or an event or during day-to-day work.

Game Summary

The team watches a video or a presentation and immediately shares their reactions via group texting. You can use this at conferences and other events to form small teams. Because this channel is private, it allows the teams a lot of latitude—especially if they are discreet in making sure other people are not seeing their texts. In addition, the team can build stronger connections as well as a technology system that can handle challenges immediately because they communicate so frequently.

Setup

Download the tool on every teammate's phone and connect all teammates into the conversation by building a group.

Instructions to the Audience

This is backchannel. We have established a group texting function that allows us to stay connected and provide our immediate feedback on what we are seeing and learning during this experience. Our goal is to learn the best lessons by sharing our different experiences and deciding on at least one action our team is going to take based on this experience. As this presentation continues, please let the your team members know what you're thinking. We can decide after the presentation whether there are any valuable takeaways for the group.

Power Tips

This is a great way to keep each of the smaller teams connected in real time if you are running a multiteam event where members can go to different areas.

Debrief

What did you find interesting? What do you remember? What feedback was positive, and what is challenging? What do you really want to say? What is the one thing we're going to take away from these responses?

Case Study

A community in Detroit, Michigan, upgraded from a listserv, an e-mail group that you can subscribe to, to GroupMe (an app that you can download to your phone that allows you to subscribe to a group that you can send texts to and receive texts from using your cell phone) to report real-time happenings with everyone in their neighborhood. They formed the ultimate community team and used that power to stop theft, stop vandalism, and ultimately make their neighborhood a better place to live.

The following is an excerpt from their blog (an online publishing website) describing their results using GroupMe:

Crime. Drugs. Murders. Corruption. Homelessness. Crappy schools. Everything you've heard about Detroit is true.

But there's a lot you may not have heard about. Urban gardens. Bike culture. Green space development. A redeveloped riverfront. Growing neighborhoods. Arts. Music. Detroit's a long way away from Shangri-la, but small pocket neighborhoods featuring low rent are attracting young professionals who want an urban experience.

My small neighborhood, Hubbard Farms, consists of about 250 homes and has been consistently solid for over a century. That's not to say we haven't had to face up to typical urban issues on a weekly basis. Car theft and [breaking and entering] are common. The infamous Hotel Yorba, a pay-by-the-week rental behemoth, sits at one end of the neighborhood. This is the last chance for most of the people there to have a roof over their heads. Many are fine citizens. But once in a while, you get some meatball who makes or draws trouble.

The neighborhood has a well-used listserv but e-mail communication is not the best way to communicate emergencies. We wanted to reach each other faster, and GroupMe gave us the answer thanks to group texting.

Since March, we've been able to stop a home invasion, interrupt a car theft in progress, and snap a clear photograph of a vagrant chucking bricks through picture windows – all thanks to our ability to amass a large number of persons very quickly to the scene of the action.

GroupMe has given our community a sense of empowerment. We know that we always have dozens of eyes and ears on the street. And if there is trouble, we know our neighbors are just a text message away. Detroit has a long way to go, but with communities using technology that supports the more positive efforts, we are just that much closer to where we all want to see things go. Better.

—Bob

Source: http://blog.groupme.com/post/6627944783/
neighborhood-watch-group-uses-groupme-to-stop

Group Texting Apps

GroupMe: http://groupme.com

Beluga: http://belugapods.com/

Facebook Messenger: http://www.facebook.com/mobile/messenger

Fast Society: http://fastsociety.com/

Team Pecha Kucha (peh-chak-cha—)Team Presentation with 20 Slides for 20 Seconds Each

Time: 40–120 minutes

Participants: 2–64; unlimited for audience; teams of 2–8 people each (4 ideal)

Technology: PowerPoint or other presentation software, Web conferencing service or projector

Category: Communication, creativity, teamwork, presentation

Goals

Have a team with anywhere from two to eight members plan and present a presentation that has 20 slides that show for 20 seconds each.

Game Summary

This is a great way to debrief a team-building initiative or get a team to work on a presentation in a short amount of time. A helpful by-product is that you can record and post this event as a way of sharing best practices or information. This rapid-fire format is perfect for attention deficit audiences and those who fear "death by PowerPoint." Results range from hilarious to pure genius.

Setup

Queue up the Pecha Kucha video, and send the accompanying template to every team leader. Set up a meeting using a Web conferencing site that can display PowerPoint slides, or, for an internal group, set up a projector.

Instructions to the Audience

(Show the video about Pecha Kucha.) Each team will have 30 minutes (or some fixed amount of time) to plan and create a Pecha Kucha on [name a particular topic; some possibilities are team building, team updates, solutions for a team challenge, leadership lessons, etc.]. Then be prepared to present to all teams when done. Points will be awarded for presentation, content, team participation, and creativity. Any questions? Go!

Case Study

Three Stony Brook University College of Leadership and Service students—Mahak Chand, Matthew Gustavson, and Michele Knabbe—used Pecha Kucha to present their case study on how their team used Web 2.0 technology to overcome virtual distance. The three students worked together to select slides, record voice-overs, compile it all, and upload it as a video—all while living in three different places! They were able to produce a great result despite their geographic differences. They used a shared website to create communal team values, used Facebook to interact with one another, used ooVoo to create three-way video conferences, and used Twitter to stay connected and get feedback from other classmates. This is pretty impressive to show in a 400-second video!

Helpful Resources

Definition: http://en.wikipedia.org/wiki/Pecha_Kucha

http://www.youtube.com/watch?v=9NZOt6BkhUg&feature=related

National Speakers Association Texas President does a Pecha Kucha on Pecha Kucha: http://www.speaker.org/video/pechakucha.html

Photo: http://nearlyzeroenergy.files.wordpress.com/2011/05/pechakuchaweb.jpg

Pecha Kucha template: http://newlearning.wordpress.com/2010/07/06/pecha-kucha-template/

Video of three students working together: http://www.youtube.com/watch?v=A7-0BW5MrWU

PowerPoint Karaoke—Team Improvisation by Presenting Slide Decks They Haven't Seen

Time: 30–120 minutes

Participants: 2–120; unlimited for audience

Technology: PowerPoint or other presentation software, Web conferencing service or projector

Category: Communication, creativity, teamwork, presentation

Goals

As a team, present a slide deck that the rest of the group has never seen before.

Game Summary

Billed as the "Newest Form of Corporate Embarrassment" by trendhunter.com, this is a great initiative for improvisation and a way to work with the information that other teams give you under tight deadlines. It also shows you how your team can set up another team for success or for failure. Best of all, it's fun and funny; you're likely to find yourself in tears of laughter at least once during this event.

Setup

Queue up the video for PowerPoint Karaoke, and make sure every team has at least one computer with PowerPoint on it. Set up a projector or a Web conferencing space using a site such as BuddyMeeting.com for the presentations.

Instructions to the Audience

You know what karaoke is, right? People who sing a song over music. Well, this is PowerPoint Karaoke, where you present on a slide deck you've never seen before. Your team will put together 10 slides and a random team will be selected to present that slide deck in 5 minutes or less. We'll give points for flow, gestures, jargon, credibility, and of course, completion (that is, getting through all the slides). You have 20 minutes to put together 10 slides, and then we'll begin presentations.

Debrief

What roles or tactics did your team use to design the slides? How did your team deal with an unknown presentation from another team? Did you feel supported or set up to fail?

Case Study

We used PowerPoint Karaoke as part of the Northwest Event Show, and it was great to watch what teams did with the various slides and presentations. Some slide decks were cohesive and helped the speaker with a presentation, whereas other teams placed random slides next to each other, knocking the presenter for a loop each time he or she advanced. What was impressive was that the best presenters were able to take a difficult slide deck and make it fantastic (see, for example, 0:22 of the PowerPoint Karaoke video). On the other hand, we saw one challenged presenter just read each slide on a slide deck about what *not* to do during a PowerPoint presentation . . . read every slide!

Sample Videos
PowerPoint Karaoke: http://www.youtube.com/watch?v=V2EbgsGkoY4
SXSW Battle Decks: http://www.trendhunter.com/trends/powerpoint-karaoke

CHAPTER
3

Trust

Trust each other again and again. When the trust level gets high enough, people transcend apparent limits, discovering new and awesome abilities for which they were previously unaware.

—David Armistead

Trust is one of the core foundations for team building. With trust, teams can go faster, soar higher, offer help when someone is falling behind, and achieve goals far beyond what any individual can do. Without trust, teams stagnate, cover their tracks, withhold information, form silos, and even sabotage their own members.

Although genuine trust is built in day-to-day interactions, trust-building games can help magnify this trust. These games are a useful diagnostic tool to discern the current level of trust within the group. In addition to diagnosis, you can use these games to identify what actions are necessary to build trust—and conversely, to figure out which actions quickly destroy it. The best definition of *trust* I have is: "Do what you say"—and these games will help your team do just that.

Last Team Texting—Trusting and Sharing Valuable Information

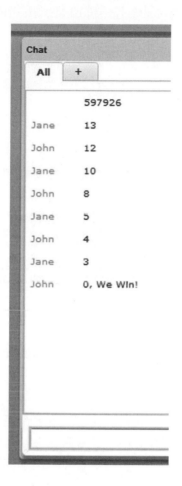

Time: 10–30 minutes

Participants: 2–4 per team; unlimited teams

Technology: chat, text, Twitter, e-mail

Category: Trust

Goals

Show how trusting and sharing valuable information with your team can increase overall success.

Game Summary

This is a fast activity where a team starts with 13 and the next team can subtract 1, 2, or 3 until a team that texts 0 wins. This game has a Power to Win Every Time secret that, once shared, can guarantee a team a win.

Setup

Divide groups of 2 to 8 into two teams, called As and Bs. Make sure each team has a way to communicate with the other team—either via chat, text, Twitter, or e-mail. Have the Power to Win Every Time information presented below ready to be exhibited on a slide or shared with the group (another option is to share on a piece of paper).

Power to Win Every Time
1. When given the possibility to text 8, always text 8.
2. When given the possibility to text 4, always text 4.
3. Always text 0 for the win.
4. If you go second, you can always win if you subtract 1 and text 12.

Instructions to the Audience

The goal of this game is to text the opposing team a 0, making your team the winner. The A team will start by texting 13 to the B team. The B team can subtract 1, 2, or 3 from the number and text the new number back to team A. Teams take turns until one team can text 0 to the other team to win.

Facilitator Notes

As the person with the knowledge, it can be fun to get a group of pairs to play the game a few times and then play the winners yourself. The point is not to show off or frustrate people; the goal is to demonstrate that having the right information is what makes you successful in many situations. It's great to hand the Power to Win Every Time information to a losing team and then let them play so they can win.

Power Tips

You can do this simple text initiative over texting phones, e-mail, a chat window in an online presentation tool, Facebook, a Twitter chat, by using only body language over a video conference, or any other creative way to transmit a number.

An additional Power Tip would be to create and send 14 photos (from 13 objects to 0 objects) that are themed to the team's objectives (such as automobiles for a car manufacturer, shoes for a shoe manufacturer, or client faces for a sales team) to each team.

Debrief

What did you think of the game when you first played? If you were given the Power to Win, what did you do with that information? Did you use it? Did you share it? What information do you or your team have that is like the Power to Win? Do you share it? If you have shared it, what results have you produced? If you don't share it, why? And what benefits could you produce if you did share it? What risks do you face if you do share it? What will you do differently based upon playing this game?

Variations

Keep track of all the A and B wins. After three to five rounds, send the Power to Win Every Time information to all team As and see if they change their behavior, such as negotiating to go second. As the facilitator, play the top-scoring team and always go second.

Case Study[1]

Sam Sikes used this activity when he was on a break at a workshop. He said it helped him convince a company's decision maker that he might have valuable information that he should trust and share with their people about how to work more efficiently as teams. After watching his team and himself play this game, the company's decision maker went on to share valuable information and make a significant impact on the company.

Trust Grid—Mapping Team Trust

Time: 20–60 minutes

Participants: 2–1,000; maximum team size of 16

Technology: Google Docs Spreadsheet or Excel with Web conference screen sharing, e-mail, text, chat

Category: Trust

Goals

Measure and learn the level of trust between team members and create a map to help identify who has high trust and why, and who has low trust and what you can do to improve it.

---

[1]*Source:* Sikes, S. *Executive Marbles and Other Team Building Activities.* (Tulsa, OK: Learning Unlimited Corporation, 1998), 104.

Game Summary

Trust Grid is a great way to visually measure a team's overall trust and determine what challenges the team faces in this area. This easy initiative asks team members to rate their level of trust with other members. If they haven't yet established a sense of trust, a team member can send his or her trust numbers directly to the facilitator. If trust has been established, you can have the team members share their feedback using a shared application such as Google Docs Spreadsheet.

Setup

Open the Trust Grid spreadsheet. A Trust Grid example can be found at http://tinyurl.com/trustgrid.

Have a private line of communication such as e-mail or text set up between you and all teammates, and give all the team members numbers from 1 to *x*.

Instructions to the Audience

Let's find out how much we trust one another on this team. On a scale of 1 to 10—with 1 indicating that you don't trust someone at all and 10 indicating that you trust someone with your life—I want you to rate your level of trust with your teammates. Everyone has received a number from 1 to *x*. Your results will be anonymous, so you can feel comfortable being completely honest in your trust rating of fellow team members. Place an M next to your own number. For instance, if I was team member 3, my entry would look like: 9, 9 M, 8, 7, 8, 6, 7 . . .

I will compile the results and share some overall results.

Power Tips

Ask the questions in the Debrief section at the beginning and at the end of the training, and see if you can increase your numbers by the end. If you have an established sense of trust on your team, then you can use Google Docs or another shared app so that everybody can see each person's rankings.

Debrief

What was the overall score for level of trust among team members? Which team member is most trusted, and why? Which team member is least trusted, and why? What would members want to see happen in order for a "trust rating" to increase? What relationships are the strongest? In other words, which team members have the highest levels of trust between them? What relationships could be strengthened? What would have to happen for those relationships to be strengthened?

Case Study

We completed a Trust Grid during a competitive and collaborative team-building event between five different teams. Each team underwent a simulation where the team had to find a balance between competition and collaboration; the team members were then asked to complete the Trust Grid again. What we didn't tell them was that one-third of their score was based on how high the other teams rated *them*. Teams that employed overly aggressive tactics to achieve a high score received low trust ratings, especially if they had to break a deal with another team to achieve that high score. Teams that worked with other teams, shared information, and helped them out achieved high trust scores.

This exercise was meant to serve as a metaphor for this especially aggressive technology company. The facilitators wanted to convey the message that although being competitive can help you achieve a short-term goal, it can hurt you in the long run, especially when working with other teams in the future. This Trust Grid launched a significant conversation about trust between teams; in the end, all teams agreed to be more collaborative so that they could join together to take market share from their biggest competitor.

The Johari Window—Discover Team Blind Spots

Time: 10–30 minutes

Participants: 1–15 per team

Technology: Internet browser

Category: Trust

Goals

By taking an assessment and having others assess you, you can discover how others view you and how that matches your perceptions of self. This can strengthen team members and a team by realizing outside perceptions and hidden gifts.

Game Summary

The Johari Window was invented by Joseph Luft and Harrington Ingham in the 1950s as a model for mapping personality awareness. By using a fixed list of adjectives, such as bold, confident, extroverted, and energetic to describe yourself and then asking your friends and colleagues to do the same, you can build a grid of overlap and difference.

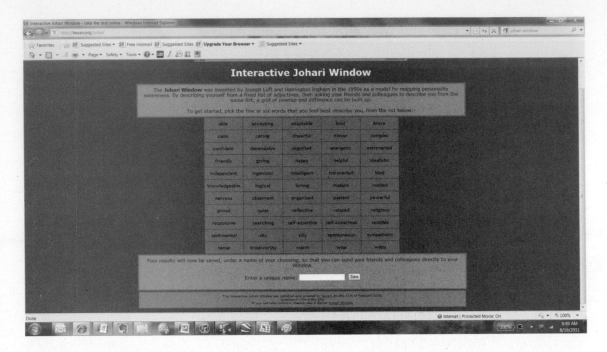

This personality awareness can help individual team members learn more about how their teammates see them and can develop teamwide awareness of strengths and weaknesses. This is a great initiative to take with newly formed teams or as a precursor to finding out how to increase team effectiveness by picking best roles for members.

Setup

Send the following link to your participants: http://kevan.org/johari. You can accelerate the process by selecting unique names to use on this website and then send the links to all of your participants. You can also attempt to do all of this online, and then compile the results into an online presentation and spend time evaluating the results.

Instructions to the Audience

The Johari Window was invented by Joseph Luft and Harrington Ingham in the 1950s as a model for mapping personality awareness. By describing yourself from a fixed list of adjectives, then asking your friends and colleagues to describe you using the same list, you can develop a grid of overlap and difference. You'll learn of your Arena (the traits of which you and others are aware), your Blind Spots (those of which you and others are not aware), your Façades (those traits that others are aware of but you aren't), and the Unknown (the traits not known by you and not known by others).

You'll start by entering your unique name and selecting five to six words that best describe you. Once you've completed that, you can then click through your teammate's links and choose five to six words that describe them. Take only 2 minutes per teammate, and then signal me when you're done. We'll then review each team member's results.

During the review period, each team member can choose a goal to increase or decrease the size of a pane. For instance, let's say that you choose to diminish your Blind Spot trait (that is, those traits that others are aware of, but you're not). You'll want to seek feedback from the group and take action that utilizes this trait in the next team activity so that you become aware of it.

Another worthy team goal is learning how to balance the giving and receiving of feedback. The Ideal window would be for each member to have a large Arena window. This represents a high degree of trust and indicates that the group has developed a known group norm by giving and receiving feedback in an effective way.

	Known to Self	Not Known to Self
Known to Others	**Arena** adaptable **energetic** giving **intelligent** knowledgeable powerful	**Blind Spot** able accepting **bold** caring cheerful clever confident **extroverted** friendly idealistic independent ingenious mature observant organised proud reflective self-assertive sentimental silly spontaneous warm wise
Not Known to Others	**Façade**	**Unknown** brave calm complex dependable dignified happy helpful introverted kind logical loving modest nervous patient quiet relaxed religious responsive searching self-conscious sensible shy sympathetic tense trustworthy witty

Power Tips

This game can be deceptively difficult. A power tip may allow people more than 2 minutes per teammate to allow more contemplation time per teammate.

If you have a cynical team or you want to explore the dark side of your team, you can use the inverse The Nohari Window, which describes your failings from a list of adjectives. Send the following link to your participants: http://kevan.org/nohari.

Debrief

How easy or challenging was it to choose your adjectives? How easy or challenging was it to choose your teammate's adjectives? What were your thoughts on choosing your teammate's adjectives? How did you narrow a person down to 5 to 6 adjectives? What did you learn from this process? What could you do differently based upon seeing the results of your assessment?

Case Study

A facilitator named Tim O'Malley introduced this tool to us during one of our own team-building retreats. This exercise helped me discover that although I was able to get one of my top three traits (intelligent) into the Arena, the other two traits (confident and extroverted) were in my Blind Spot. I set a goal of reducing my Blind Spot by attempting to be more confident and extroverted during our next team-led project. I was unaware as a group leader that my confidence was a crucial trait I could use to move a project forward. And although I knew I was extroverted, I also looked to purposefully talk less during some team meetings to make sure other voices could be heard. Taking these actions allowed our next team project to go more smoothly than they had in the past. If you'd like to review my personal results or contribute to my Johari's Window, visit http://kevan.org/johari?name=bigkid.

Video Matching and Mirroring—Build Instant Team Rapport

> Time: 5–30 minutes
> Participants: 4–12
> Technology: Skype, video conference service
> Category: Trust

Goals

Build rapport between teammates by successfully mirroring the leader's actions.

Game Summary

Video Matching and Mirroring uses a traditional technique for creating rapport by getting the team to follow a leader's movements and gestures. This can also help the team become more aware of their video presence when they are videoconferencing.

Setup

Connect all teams by video conference using Skype, Google+ Hangouts, ooVoo, or another multiperson video conference.

Instructions to the Audience

Today we're going to work on team rapport. Science tells us that more than 58 percent of our communication is conveyed via body language and that you can create rapport and enhance trust with others by matching and mirroring another person's gestures, from the obvious motions such as arm placement and hand gestures to more subtle body language such as the rate of someone's breathing or their facial expressions. We're going to participate in an exercise where we each take a turn as leader, and everyone else must match our actions. Everyone will take turns being the leader for a time period of 1 minute.

Debrief

What motions and poses did we make? Which ones were enjoyable? Which ones were uncomfortable? How did we compare to the average of conveying 58 percent of communication through body language? Do you feel you have a stronger rapport with the other person? Why or why not? What can we learn to do differently from this exercise? What will we commit to do in the next 30 days?

Variations

A variation is the game Dance to the Beat of a Different Drummer. For this game, play 1 minute of different songs to signal when to switch leaders. This can result in hilarious dance moves.

Case Study

Rapport is the relationship of mutual understanding or trust and agreement between people. In a more advanced version of this exercise, each team consisted of three people. One person imagined and acted out an emotionally intense experience. The second person attempted to match that person's body position, breathing, and muscle tension as much as possible. The third person coached the second person on how to move or change to match the first person exactly. When I was the second person attempting to match the first person, I had *no* idea what she was imagining. After 5 minutes of getting into and holding this position, I guessed that she was in a white building, kneeling toward the front of the room and contemplating a significant decision. I was pretty much on the money; she disclosed after the exercise that she was in a church, praying and trying to decide if she was going to stay in her marriage. Needless to say, we were all blown away. This exercise shows that you can build strong connections between team members by matching and mirroring one another's actions.

Skype Interview—Capturing Team Knowledge through Video Interviews

Time: 5–30 minutes

Participants: 2–1,000; divided into pairs

Technology: Skype, VodBurner, teleconference or live meeting service

Category: Trust

Goals

Create connection and increase trust among team members by videoing an interview. In addition, videos can be posted to continue building connection and trust among team members who are not in the video.

Game Summary

Skype Interview is a great breakout team-building event in which team members can use one-on-one conversations to build relationships and trust. In addition, using a free Skype recorder allows you to edit and upload the video and share the interview results with the entire team.

Setup

Make sure that the Skype video recording software you're using is installed properly. I have used the free version of VodBurner, available at http://www.vodburner.com/, to successfully record interviews; however, be aware that this program can make some very large files in recording your conversation. Encourage each person to be in a quiet location and have a working video camera, speakers/headset, and microphone; ensure that there is enough bandwidth for the number of people on the call. Group teammates into pairs and check that you have an easy way to share the other person's Skype ID. Use a central YouTube or other video-sharing tool or server to which you can upload videos. Develop powerful questions to ask during the interview and send to all participants.

Instructions to the Audience

Today we will break into pairs and get a chance to interview one of our teammates. I've sent a list of all the people who are calling and those who will be receiving the call. Make sure your recording software is turned on and then spend approximately half of the time with the first person answering the questions and half of the time waiting for the other person to answer. When you're done, you can hang up and click the Share button to upload your video to the account we sent you. Then we will meet back in this room or teleconference to discuss what we all learned.

Sample Questions:

Can you tell me about the best team you've worked on—and why it was the best?

What did you do before this job?

What's the biggest work success you've had, and what role did you have in it?

What's the most challenging work situation you've faced, and how did you handle it?

What's the biggest mistake you've made in the past? How did you get past it?

Power Tips

Use Trust Grid before and after this exercise; early studies have shown trust levels to increase after conducting this kind of video interview.

Create a contest for the best interview by having participants vote on other videos. The bonus effect is having teammates meet other teammates virtually though the online videos and learn something about them.

Debrief

What happened during your interview? What did you learn about your teammate that you didn't know before? How much more or less do you trust this person after this interview? What will you now do differently when working with this teammate?

Case Study

During the Green Meetings Industry Council's 2011 conference, we were able to recruit team members who were watching a live video broadcast while on Twitter. We brought one member named Samuel J. Smith into our meeting via Skype, and he became a fully contributing team member. After the team meeting, I called Sam to interview him about his experience; we all thought it was very cool that this had just happened without any advance planning. We recorded the interview, and I posted it on YouTube immediately afterward.

When I ran into the conference organizer that evening and told her this story, she asked if we could show the interview at the morning opening. I cut a 2-minute version of the video that was played to more than 200 meeting participants. Even more important, Samuel and I have become good friends after bumping into each other on Twitter and virtual conferences, even though we still have not yet met face to face!

To view the entire interview with Samuel J. Smith, visit http://www.youtube.com/watch?v=i1MUy0qQxNM.

Improving Performance

The greatest gain a team can make in efficiency is enhancing communication between members and teams. Teams can speed up a process by 50 percent or more, simply by improving their communication, trust, and team process. The games in this chapter focus on improving a team's performance in completing a complex task. A simple stopwatch lets you create a tangible improvement in team performance by using these and many other initiatives. In a time when it seems like teams are continually being asked to do more with less, team process is the most promising area in which improvement can be made.

These games are exciting and popular because they can produce tangible results. In addition, if you use the same process the game highlights with a work process, the team can make similar gains in a professional setting that they do during the game. One team decreased the time it took to complete a challenge from 7:24 to 2:37—a 65 percent reduction. Another case study shows how a team used this process to turn a 4-hour process into a 3-second push of a button with no additional work. This kind of enhanced production will boost your team's morale and compel them to make significant wins in their work.

A to Z—The A to Z of Building and Speeding Up Team Process

Time: 5–30 minutes

Participants: 4–12

Technology: Chat, text

Category: Improving performance

Goals

Examine and improve team process to chat the letters A through Z without having anyone chat the same letter twice, restarting if any mistake is made.

Game Summary

A to Z is a very simple team-building game that can quickly assess your team's ability to create a process and iterate to accelerate that process.

Setup

Connect all teams via chat and teleconference.

Instructions to the Audience

This team-building initiative shows how a team tackles a challenge while working online. The team needs to chat A through Z as fast as possible, and no person can chat twice in a row. If any letter is entered out of order, the team needs to start back at A. There is no talking when you're being timed during this initiative.

Power Tips

A possible solution is for 2 people in a 3 or more person team to just chat back and forth. You can reward this creative solution and add an additional rule that every person needs to be involved or go further that each teammate needs to do about an equal amount of work.

Debrief

How did our team tackle this challenge? What does this say about our team process? What can we do to improve our team process? How would we approach this challenge if we were to do it again?

Variations

You can repeat this initiative up to two more times, timing each iteration. Allow 2 to 5 minutes for planning before you start the stopwatch. Write down the times for each completion and calculate the percentage increase or decrease in time. Usually, a team can reduce its time by as much as 20 to 80 percent just by tweaking its team process.

Case Study

I completed this initiative during a training event for volunteers of an organization to help them become better leaders. One team in particular clearly displayed their skills in the first two rounds by achieving the fastest time. In the third round, a new team that was almost in last place jumped to first; they were able to cut their time in half and come in with the fastest time out of the three timed trials. When I interviewed them afterward, they told me the secret of their success: to take a risk on a new process that could create a big jump in speed. Although they had given it some thought during the second round, they were too afraid that it would fail and they would end up in last place. However, they decided during the final round that they didn't want to play *not* to lose; they wanted to *play to win*. They practiced the new technique to prove it worked, and when it came to an actual timed trial, they nailed it! They learned from this experience that although you can make small incremental improvements, you sometimes need to abandon your previous process and invent a better one to make a quantum leap in performance. And the rewards of winning made it all worthwhile. Just by typing A to Z, these participants were able to see how a simple initiative can lead to effective team building, valuable learning, and improved performance.

Grid Unlock—Collaborative Team Problem Solving with Shared Spreadsheets

Time: 15–30 minutes

Participants: 4–12 per team

Technology: Whiteboard, Google Docs or another application that allows simultaneous editing

Category: Improving performance

Goals

Collaborate as a team to find a solution to a complex number problem to discover team problem-solving processes and learn techniques to increase team problem solving.

Game Summary

Grid Unlock is a classic magic squares challenge that's been updated to work with a team and either a whiteboard or shared document technology. This is a great initiative for analytical thinking, problem solving, communication, and cooperation that features the bonus of teaching a team how to collaborate on a single document.

Setup

Connect all teams by using a whiteboard or Google Docs to a shared spreadsheet and teleconference. Open a spreadsheet that has a 3 × 3 box containing the numbers 1 through 9 with totals for every row, column, and diagonal.

Grid Unlock Tools

Link to template Grid Unlock: http://tinyurl.com/gridunlock

Link to Grid Unlock solution: http://tinyurl.com/gridunlocksolution

Instructions to the Audience

Your team needs to rearrange the numbers in the grid to unlock the correct code—the one that has results in every row, every column, and both diagonals adding up to 15. The first team member can swap only two numbers; the next team member then swaps two numbers; and so on. You have 10 minutes to complete this challenge.

Power Tips

Here are hints you can give to a stuck team or a team looking to improve performance. You can give these hints one at a time until a team achieves the result.

Write the digit 5 in the center block.

9, 1, 5 and 9, 2, 4 are the only sets of digits that work for 9, so write 9 in a non-corner spot.

Write 1 across from 9.

Write 4 and 2 in the corner squares next to 9.

Write 6 across from 4.

Write 8 across from 2.

Fill in 3 and 7 to complete the puzzle.

Debrief

How did our team tackle this challenge? What does this say about our team process? How can we improve our team process? How would we approach this situation if we were going to do it again?

Variations

You can repeat this initiative up to two more times, timing each iteration. Give participants 2 to 5 minutes of planning time before you start the stopwatch. Write down the times for each completion and calculate the percentage increase or decrease in time.

You can also involve more people and make it more complex by creating a 4 × 4 grid that totals 34 using the numbers 1 through 16 or a 5 × 5 grid that totals 65 using the numbers 1 through 25. However, keep in mind that adding more people will slow down the problem solving and increase the chaos.

Case Study

This game truly provides teams with key lessons on planning, accepting failure, and using all your resources to create the best end result. This team approached Grid Unlock like most other teams did; they used trial and error and took more than 12 minutes to complete the entire task. During the debrief, they agreed that they wanted to improve their performance. One team member asked what the fastest time was in which anybody had finished this challenge, which was about 2 seconds. Although there was only 5 minutes of planning time for the second stage, the team realized they had three attempts and they *all* agreed to spend all the planning and execution time for the second attempt in figuring out the 2-second solution, thus giving themselves a poorer time during the second attempt. They had determined each team member's role and were all clear on the plan. When the clock started, every team member filled in his or her one to two boxes and called time. In just 1.87 seconds, they had completed the magic square—reducing their execution time by 99.7 percent! The debriefing period taught the team members how to ask game-changing questions, how to have the courage to "fail" during a trial to "win" the event goal, and how to approach future projects with the mind-set to radically succeed.

Marshmallow Challenge—Build a Tower, Build a Team

Time: 45–60 minutes

Participants: 4–1,000, divided into teams of 4

Technology: Skype, video conference

Category: Improving performance

Goals

Teams improve team design, team process, and team prototyping skills to build the highest freestanding tower in a limited time period using 20 sticks of spaghetti, 1 yard of tape, 1 yard of string, and 1 marshmallow, which must be on top of the tower.

Game Summary

The Marshmallow Challenge is the best TED (Technology, Entertainment, Design) team-building video in that it puts forth a very simple challenge and provides great research about how best to approach teamwork. This team-building initiative teaches the power of *proto-typing*, the process of creating many successful models along the way instead of just one. It can also convey important lessons about risk versus reward and how to best work in a team that designs new solutions.

Setup

Per Team

20 unbroken sticks of spaghetti

1 yard of masking tape

1 yard of string

1 large marshmallow

1 countdown timer

1 tape measure

TED Video

Connect all teams via video conference using Skype, Google+ Hangouts, ooVoo, or another multiperson video conference, one conference per team. Make sure each team has a leader who brought all the building materials (20 sticks of spaghetti, 1 yard of tape, 1 yard of string, and 1 marshmallow); also, have a countdown timer set to 18 minutes (you can find one at http://www.online-stopwatch.com/) and have a tape measure to measure height. Have the TED video ready to play and be prepared to share your screen with all other teams. You can also download the PowerPoint slides from the website to help present the information.

Instructions to the Audience

You have been placed in (or have formed) teams of four. Each team will have 18 minutes to build the tallest freestanding structure that has the marshmallow on top of 20 sticks of spaghetti, using 1 yard of tape and 1 yard of string. Are there any questions? (Address any questions.) Go!

■ ■ ■

At the end of 18 minutes, instruct every team to measure their tower's height and reward the top team.

Then play the TED video to begin the debrief.

Power Tips

I carry an iPad or other note-taking device and place timing marks such as 16:05, Team 5 is still talking, 14:10 Team 3 completes first small prototype of a working tower. These notes are useful in the debrief to remember significant events for a team and ask them what they were thinking about at that time. You can also capture key quotes from teams such as "This is impossible," which can also be used in the debrief.

If you are interested in the highest solution, you need to think in triangles. In addition, one of the best solutions at over 39 inches is to use 3 or 4 spaghetti sticks at the bottom, working your way to 1 spaghetti stick at the top and build a flat 2-dimensional structure. Then use the string to tape to the table and lean the structure by attaching the string to the middle of the tower. This allows for more material than a pyramid solution, and other teams are amazed at the out-of-the-box solution that they did not think of.

Debrief

What did we do with our time? What was our general approach? When did we put the marshmallow on? How many working prototypes did we complete? How did we compare with the averages? How do we feel about that? What can we learn to do differently from this exercise? What will we commit to do in the next 30 days?

Case Study

After conducting more than 70 of these events, the best conclusion we've drawn is that, on average, kindergartners build higher structures than do MBA graduates!

We used the Marshmallow Challenge to teach students engaged in a robotics competition about iterative design. Nine students were divided into three teams, and two teams fell into the typical "uh-oh" patterns; in other words, they left the marshmallow until the end and both of their towers collapsed at the end of the 18 minutes. One team had a member who had done the exercise before, and she was able to work with her other two teammates to create a triangular tower that was 22 inches high.

The entire team watched the 7-minute YouTube video after building towers, and each student was able to commit to tangible actions that helped them in the upcoming weeks during the final debrief. The first success occurred the very next week, when each subteam was able to demo a working prototype; during previous weeks, they had spent time talking and failed to produce any actual prototypes. This team went on to place fifth and win the highly coveted and most prestigious of all awards, the Inspire award for overall performance, and the Marshmallow Challenge was mentioned by the judges as one of the reasons why they chose this team. The Inspire award immediately qualifies this team for state competition.

This team-building initiative can be conducted live or using video conference and has a lot of supporting information and materials that create a great learning event.

Helpful Resources

7 Minute TED Talk by Tom Wujec http://www.ted.com/talks/tom_wujec_build_a_tower.html

Tom Wujec's blog site with resources and recent stories of The Marshmallow Challenge http://marshmallowchallenge.com

Seattle Academy of Arts and Science's (SAAS) Robotics team qualifies for state championship with the use of The Marshmallow Challenge http://www.seattleacademy.info/wp/sector-saas-qualifies-for-state-competition/

Customized Jeopardy—Test Teams' Retention of Information

Time: 10–30 minutes

Participants: 2–4 per team; 2–10 teams

Technology: Internet, Web Conferencing

Category: Improving performance

Goals

To increase team performance by increased retention of key information through a competitive game show format.

Game Summary:

Jeopardy is a classic game to test trivia or memory retention. This team-building game is perfect after teaching a section on a given topic and attempting to determine who has retained the most information.

Setup

Go to http://www.superteachertools.com/jeopardy/index.php, one of the better online Jeopardy game setups. (This one doesn't require PowerPoint, and it also comes in a stand-alone version.) Select Make a New Game by clicking the following:

This allows you to input up to 25 questions and answers, and it even shows you how to insert pictures from the Internet for visual clues. Save the game as a .txt file, or copy the link to be able to play this game online:

Finally, set up a teleconference and PIN number. Log in to buddymeeting.com; start a new meeting and fill in the information:

Next, click Create, copy the information, and send it to all participants with the link to http://buddymeeting.com/join.php, along with information on the date and time to log in. Then click on Start Meeting 15 to 30 minutes prior to starting.

When the meeting starts, click 🖥 on the top left of buddymeeting.com to share your screen. Then click Full Screen, and switch to the screen with Jeopardy on it.

Instructions to the Audience

Welcome to Customized Jeopardy, where we give you the answers and you give us the questions. We have set up teams to play today; you can simply buzz in by calling out your name, and I will call on you. (You can also substitute the text window to buzz in if you arrange your windows to be able to see the text window.) This round will feature a Daily Double, and then we'll tackle Final Jeopardy. Are you ready? Let's play!

Power Tips

This version of Jeopardy has built-in sound effects that you can turn off by using a control located in the bottom right-hand corner when the game board is showing. It allows you to click through the screens quickly; you can click on the question, wait for the answer, and then click Answer. Click Adjust Scores and Correct for the team who got it right, and click Wrong for any team who got it wrong. Then click Home to go back to the board.

You can use other versions of screen sharing (such as Skype) if they react faster than BuddyMeeting. Some locations may have a delay, so be sure to read the question like a game host would; this guarantees that participants will hear the question before their screen catches up.

Debrief

Did you use all the different resources on your team to increase your score? What did you learn from the other teams during this event? What could your team do to further increase retention?

Case Study

A hotel manager started using Customized Jeopardy after he'd completed a customer service training section. Because the manager did not announce the first session, the teams scored very few points; it turned out that they were not paying close attention during the training. Once this information came to light, each team began using multiple retention techniques, such as taking notes, using mnemonic devices, and testing each other before the game. The scores more than doubled during the next game—and more important, the manager was able to test and measure higher use of the training during work hours as reflected by increasing guest card scores and secret shopper reports after the training session was completed. The manager—and subsequently, the entire hotel chain—went on to win a monthly award for greatest improvement in customer service, further boosting the team's morale and getting them noticed by headquarters.

QR Scavenger Hunt—Scan Your Way to Team Building

Time: 30–120 minutes

Participants: 2–12 per team; infinite teams

Technology: Smartphone, QR code scanner

Category: Improving performance

Goals

Increase team performance through solving challenges, viewing videos, learning company information, or learning a new company skill through the use of a competitive QR (Quick Response) code scavenger hunt.

Game Summary

QR (Quick Response) codes are placed in various locations on products, signs, publications, and other sources. You can use a smartphone app to scan these and bring up a URL, text message, phone number, or an SMS (Short Message Service or a cell phone-based text message) ready to send. It's easy to create a scavenger hunt by creating a collection of QR codes with a generator. You can challenge teams to learn a new technology and solve a variety of problems that can teach your teams any collection of knowledge or skills you want them to learn or develop.

Setup

Define the goal of the scavenger hunt (to take them to specific areas, for them to learn a new skill, etc.). Then design what you want the team to experience or do at each site. The QR code can take you to a website, play a video, call a phone number, and listen to a message—all of which can help you achieve your overall goal. Assign a point value and design a question for each location that members can answer only by scanning the QR code to verify that their team was there.

For instance, let's say you want the teams to learn about the definition of team building. The Wikipedia entry on team building is available at http://en.wikipedia.org/wiki/Team_building. From this definition, I create the question "What is the first reason for team building?" Based on the entry, the correction answer should be "Improving communication." I write this in a spreadsheet and give it a point value of 500 points so that I have room for easier and more challenging locations. I decide to hide this QR code in the lunchroom, so I add the clue "Food for thought."

Food for thought: What is the first reason for team building?	Lunch room	Improving communication	500

Next I go to http://qrcode.kaywa.com to create the QR code. I cut and paste http://en.wikipedia.org/wiki/Team_building into the URL and click Generate! Once I've made my QR code, I right-click on the QR code and select Save Image As . . . and save it into a directory. I give this one the name Lunchroom.php so I can remember where it goes. Then I print it out in large format and hide it in the lunchroom.

Another option is to create a score sheet for each team that contains an entry for each QR code location and the correct answer. Each location entry should display a clue about the location, the question, a space for an answer, the point value, and a space to mark off whether the response was correct.

Clue	Answer	Points	Correct
Food for thought: What is the first reason for team building?		500	

You can also set up QR codes in different locations of a room and create stations that every team needs to complete. (*Note:* There are several kinds of systems emerging that will track the teams that have been to a site; however, I have not been able to use one successfully for an event.) Create a key that contains the correct answers to make it easy to quickly score the answer sheets. Send an e-mail instructing at least one person from each team to download a QR code scanner such as Kaywa (http://qrcode.kaywa.com) to his or her smartphone.

Instructions to the Audience

This is a QR code scavenger hunt, so let's make sure each team has at least one phone with a working scanner. (Have each team scan a test QR code to ensure that all systems are working.) Your team needs to complete as many missions as possible by finding and scanning the QR code and answering the question. The score sheet has hints about where the QR code is hidden, what the question is, a space for the right answer, and finally, how many points the correct answer is worth. You must return by the specified time or your team will be disqualified—and you must have the correct answer to score. Your return time is [specify a return time]. Go!

Debrief

What strategy (if any) did your team set out to use? What actually happened in the field? Who do you know better from participating in this event? What will you do differently with your team now? How can your team more effectively balance planning and doing? How can you better assign roles and goals to maximize your team's results? What do you need to do to maximize one of your underutilized resources (e.g., making sure to ask the quiet members of the group for their opinions after discovering a challenge to see if they know the answer)?

Case Study

A librarian wanted to create a team-building event for her ESOL (English for Speakers of Other Languages) kids, so she took an old scavenger hunt and used a collection of tools to upgrade it and create custom QR codes. The missions she assigned included finding a recipe in an Italian recipe book and looking up a word in the dictionary to get the definition. In addition to teaching the kids how to work better together, it showed them how to locate books in a section using the Dewey Decimal System, how to use a physical dictionary, as well as helping to hone other library skills.

Any scavenger hunt team-building event will help develop planning skills, group process, goals, and roles, and you can debrief those behaviors after the event to look for winning patterns.

Check out this award-winning blog to gain more ideas on how to use this activity to create a team-building event: http://www.thedaringlibrarian.com/2011/03/qr-code-quest-library-scavenger-hunt.html.

CHAPTER 5

Problem Solving

It's not that I'm so smart, it's just that I stay with problems longer.

—Albert Einstein

If you don't make mistakes, you're not working on hard enough problems.
And that's a big mistake.

—Frank Wilczek

Problem solving is a critical skill for high-performing teams. It is the culmination of team communication, elevated trust, out-of-the-box thinking, and the ability to play with new and potentially unrelated ideas until a solution is created. Teams that get "stuck" have a difficult time solving problems because they begin to believe that they simply cannot solve them. The following games are designed to get teams into the problem-solving mind-set. They aim to open team members' minds to new solutions, encourage them to listen to fellow teammates, work together as a team even if they don't understand the idea entirely, and most of all, help them recognize when they have solved a key problem and celebrate it! These games are a great starting point and way to get teams to ask, "If we can solve this, what else can we solve?"

Move One Line/Add One Line—Team Creativity with More Than One Solution

Time: 10–30 minutes

Participants: 2–8 per team; unlimited teams

Technology: Internet, Google Docs or another application that allows simultaneous editing

Category: Problem solving

Goals

Increase a team's creativity by creating as many solutions as possible to a visual puzzle by moving or adding a line.

Game Summary

This game is a classic creativity team-building challenge that's simply been moved online. Each of the two challenges has multiple potential answers. The exercise compels teams to think outside of the box and create more than one solution. This is a good way to get people in the proper mind-set when they have to tackle a real problem in the workplace.

Setup

Log in to Google Docs. Create two drawings: Save the first one as "Move One Line" and create lines to make this picture.

Create the second drawing to make these pictures and change the name to "Add One Bar." *Note:* Make sure each participant has a Google Docs account. Click the Share button. **🔒 Share**

Add their e-mail addresses to share this document. Then go to File > Make a copy:

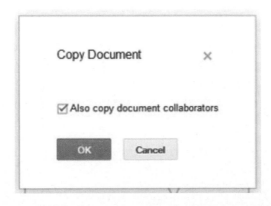

Check "Also copy document collaborators" and click OK:

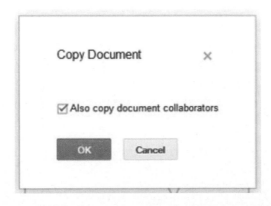

Change the document to look like this:

Click "Copy of Move One Line" to rename it:

Change the name to "Add One Line":

Rename Document   ×

Enter a new document name:

Copy of Move One Line

OK   Cancel

Then set up a teleconference line for all participants and provide instructions to log into Google Docs before the call starts. Make sure that you have a timer ready.

Instructions to the Audience

(For Move One Line) We're going to work on creativity. Log into Google Docs and open the document titled "Move One Line." You can move any of the bars below to make both sides of this equation equal. However, the equal sign is *not* a bar and therefore cannot be moved. You may consider the "V" one or two bars. Make sure you select the pointer tool (show them what it looks like: ⬆) before moving the lines.

   (Start a timer for 5 to 10 minutes, or just take a read on when the group energy starts to decline. If they get to a point where it seems like they're slowing down, you may need to suggest that there is more than one solution. Debrief this first attempt and get the group to agree to one new positive action for the next challenge.)

■ ■ ■

(For Add One Line) Let's take what we learned about creativity from the last challenge and apply it to this one. Switch documents to "Add One Line." Add one line to the IX below to turn it into a 6.

Facilitator Notes

Following, you will find the current set of solutions. If a team is able to clearly explain an answer without violating a stated rule, then compliment their creativity and send me a .jpg of their answer!

Move One Line Solutions

$$1 = \sqrt{1}$$

The line is moved to form a square root symbol over a 1, and the square root of 1 is 1.

A line is moved to form a multiplication symbol between two 1s, and 1 times 1 is 1.

$$| = \backslash \; |{\dashv}$$

A line is moved to form a subtraction symbol: II minus I is I

$$| = \nabla \; |$$

A line caps the "V" to form a triangular zero: 01 equals 1.

A line turns the "V" into an "N" to spell "nil" with the first two letters written in uppercase and the last letter written in lowercase; nil means nothing, which is what is to the left of the equal sign.

$$\slashed{} = \backslash \; ||$$

A line is moved to the left side to form an "X": "X" can equal anything, including III.

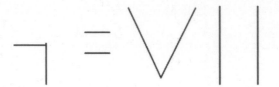

A line on the left is moved by bending it to form a seven: 7 equals Roman numeral VII. You can facilitate this solution by drawing the left line with two segments and letting the team discover that it's made of two lines.

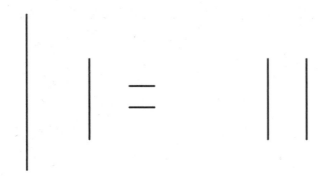

If the "V" is straightened, counted as one line and moved to the left side of the equation, you get 2 equals 2.

Add One Line Solutions

Using the scribble tool ( ), drawing a line in the shape of an "S" makes the puzzle spell six.

A line in the shape of a "6" makes the puzzle six since 1 times 6 is 6.

A straight line divides the puzzle so that it is a Roman numeral six—if you look at it upside down with its mirror image below.

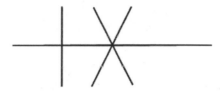

You need to know your math functions for this one. One straight line turns this into the expression of the absolute value of "X"...which can be 6.

One bent line turns the 1 into a 4; using the rules of Roman numerals, the smaller number on the left is subtracted from the larger number on the right. Roman numeral X (10) minus

Arabic number 4 equals 6. My editor of this book discovered another interpretation that I have never seen. This equation can be $4x$ where $x = 1.5$ such that $4 \times 1.5 = 6$. Now that's creative thinking on the fly and I want my editor on my team!

This expression is defined as two parallel lines and four intersecting lines; add all the lines together and it totals 6.

Debrief

How many solutions did you find before you stopped the first time? How did new ideas emerge and get accepted? What are barriers to new solutions? What are the supporting factors of new solutions? Who are the supporters of new ideas and who are the detractors? How can we apply what we learned to the next challenge we face at work?

Case Study[1]

Move One Line/Add One Line was used with a team before they tackled the issue of dealing with travel receipts. The team was taking far too long to send in receipts after a project ended; people were losing receipts or failing to send them back to headquarters for proper filing. In addition, everyone grumbled about having to complete expense reports.

After getting into the mind-set of finding solutions, the team began to rapidly bring forth new ideas. One solution was to purchase new scanner equipment and send it to every event. Since cost and weight were an issue with this, another team member suggested scanning or faxing the receipts in from the hotels; however, although this would eliminate extra equipment, it might require an additional cost if the hotel charged for a fax. Another teammate suggested having a digital camera shipped to every event so that attendees could

[1]*Sources:* Sikes, S. *Executive Marbles and Other Team Building Activities.* (Tulsa, OK: Learning Unlimited Corporation, 1998), 60.

Priest, S. & Rohnke, K. #53 and #54 of *101 of the Best Corporate Team-Building Activities,* 2nd ed. (Tacoma, WA: Tarrak Technologies, 2000). http://www.tarrak.com/BOOKS/101.htm

Priest, S., Sikes, S. & Evans, F. #48 of *99 of the Best Experiential Corporate Games We Know.* (Lakebay, WA: eXperientia, 2000). http://www.tarrak.com/BOOKS/99.htm

take photos of the receipts, download the photos to their computers, and then send the images to the accountant. Although this approach eliminated the extra cost and weight issue, it took more time than necessary—and there was still the potential for receipts to get lost between the time when someone purchased an item and when they finally got back to their computer.

Finally, one team member suggested using the cameras that employees had on their phones to immediately send a photo as an e-mail attachment to the accountant, letting the accountant know the amount, merchant, and project associated with the expense in the subject line. This solution allowed each team member to take care of the expenses at the moment of incurring the expense—and as a result, the percentage of receipts received jumped from 50 percent to more than 95 percent. In addition, since the information that employees sent in was easier to track—and they had to add in things only that were paid in cash (which they also started to send in photos of)—the reports were simpler for them to complete. This is a case where moving a line really created out-of-the-box thinking that saved thousands of dollars and hours.

Templates

Move One Line Google Docs Template: http://tinyurl.com/moveoneline

Add One Line Google Docs Template: http://tinyurl.com/addoneline

Consensus Voting—Choosing Top Team Options Online

Time: 15–30 minutes

Participants: 4–12 per team

Technology: Whiteboard, Google Docs or another application that allows simultaneous editing

Category: Problem solving

Goals

Solve team problems using a multiple voting system to help set priorities or make decisions. Teach a team a system for reaching consensus faster.

Game Summary

Consensus Voting is a great initiative to discover where a team's energies or priorities are.

Setup

Log in to Google Docs. Go to Create New > Spreadsheet.

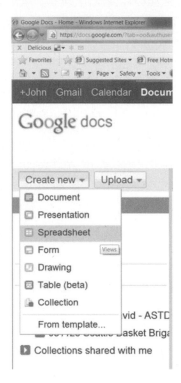

Click Share on the top right, and give the spreadsheet a name like "Consensus Voting"; click OK.

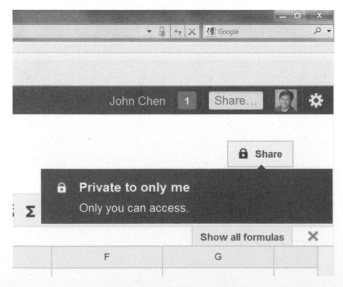

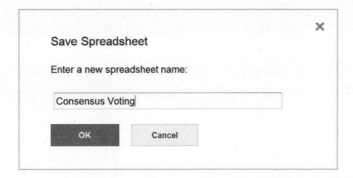

Add all of your teammates by name or by adding their e-mail addresses in the Add people box. Click Share & save, and then click Done.

Write your options in column A, starting at cell A2. In cell B1, enter "Total"; in B2, enter "=SUM(B2:N2)" and then copy B2 and paste into B3 and the cells below to match the options in column A.

Instructions to the Audience

We need to make a team decision for our next step, and we have a lot of options. I want us to think about the next decision that we believe will have the most significant impact on our project and the company overall. First, let's brainstorm our options. Each team member can add one option that covers a topic he or she considers to be most important. (Be sure to allow every team member to add an option or choose to pass. Add each option to column A, and consolidate any similar options.) Okay, now you each get five votes. I'm going to assign you to a column, and you can vote by putting the number of votes in the row of the option you choose. Start with column C and continue through letters as necessary.) We'll look at the highest-voted options and then make a team decision.

Facilitator Notes

Remember that since this vote is public and not anonymous, it might bring to light other issues about which team members are and are not supporting one another. As the facilitator, make sure that the leader, team, and company are open for this team to make any decision. If higher-level employees have already made a decision, this initiative can damage team trust and morale. You don't want to ask for a team's input and then ignore it.

Power Tips

In live versions of Consensus Voting, I have used bandannas to hide the votes and given each person 5 poker chips for their voting. In this digital team-building version, you could have teammates submit their votes anonymously by text, chat, e-mail, direct message on Twitter, or other means to keep their votes anonymous and avoid the issue of influencing future votes based upon current votes.

Debrief

Are you surprised at the result? Do you agree with the result? Can you buy into the team decision enough to support it, even if it's not your choice? If not, what has to happen to convince you to support it?

Variations

You can use fewer or more votes, ranging from 1 to 10.

Case Study

A high-impact nonprofit used Consensus Voting for a board meeting that was held in multiple locations. Although the majority of the team was face to face in the same location, two members were calling in remotely. This board needed to decide on a critical next step that could alter the distant future of the organization; in addition, the current state of the economy was putting their short-term funding in jeopardy. This board was also notorious for getting excited about a lot of new projects but not getting consensus on the critical steps needed for the organization now. We brainstormed 10 different options and came up with the following results:

1. Document rhythm of business—0 votes
2. Clarify and communicate vision and value, program definition—18 votes
3. Stabilize and increase funding—10 votes
4. Stabilize and reinvigorate all existing programs—9 votes
5. Gain feedback about sponsorships, programs, and business leads (manager)—7 votes
6. Build scalable resource model—6 votes
7. Maximize alumni—6 votes
8. Create diversity board to represent community—5 votes
9. Develop 10-year strategy—5 votes
10. Build and strengthen alliances—4 votes

Although individuals on the board were excited about smaller projects, the Consensus Voting clearly showed that the entire board needed to get back to basics by clarifying their vision and value and using that to stabilize and increase funding by attracting donors and increasing enrollment into their program. Everyone on the board agreed to these three objectives. They banded together to help one another hit key goals in these areas to end the year successfully.

Like to Move It—Quick Spatial Team Diagnosis

Time: 30–60 minutes

Participants: 2–8 per team; unlimited teams

Technology: Internet, Google Docs or another application that allows simultaneous editing

Category: Problem solving

Goals

Diagnose and improve team problem-solving skills using a spatial problem.

Game Summary

I Like to Move It is based on the classic Towers of Hanoi exercise in which a team must work together to transfer a tower of items from one location to another. This simple drill quickly reveals any communication and trust issues and is therefore a great tool for early team diagnosis.

Setup

Log in to Google Docs. Go to http://tinyurl.com/7mkl343 or create a drawing that looks like this:

Save it as "I Like to Move It." Make sure each participant has a Google account, click the Share button (🔒 Share), and add their e-mail addresses to share this document:

Set up a teleconference line for all participants and send instructions to log in to Google Docs before the call starts.

Instructions to the Audience

Your team goal is to move this stack of lines from one location to another utilizing the least number of moves. You can move only one piece at a time, and you cannot place a larger piece on top of a smaller piece in one of the three provided spaces. Make sure you select the pointer tool (▶) before moving the lines, and be sure to move only the lines. Do not resize them or change their shape.

Power Tips

You can use more or fewer lines to increase or decrease the complexity; for example, a perfect score for 4 lines = 15 moves, 5 lines = 31 moves, and 6 lines = 63 moves. Key themes that emerge from this team-building game are problem solving, communication, sharing of ideas, leadership, and analytical thinking. This activity can also be analogous to other real work activities, such as moving inventory, staging an office relocation, or undertaking a complex project such as building a product or a house.

Debrief

Did your team plan before starting? Did you get stuck at all? If so, what did you do? How would you describe the team process? Who did the most moving? Who did the least moving and why? How do you think you could speed up the process? How could you make the process more harmonious? What can we learn from this team-building process to perform better at work?

Case Study[2]

One team used this exercise before conducting a large office move. They completed the game twice with five lines. The first effort took more than 45 moves to finish. With proper planning, clear communication among team members, and assignment of key roles, they were able to achieve the minimum of 31 moves. Each teammate committed to fulfilling a key role in the debrief, such as looking for dependencies, preplanning the next four moves, and preventing violation of rules (thereby keeping safety issues in mind). They created five moving categories

---

[2]*Sources:* Priest, S. #73 of *100 of the Best Virtual Team-Building Events*. (Seattle, WA: Tarrak Technologies, 2001). virtualteamworks.com; http://www.tarrak.com/BOOKS/100.htm

Priest, S. & Rohnke, K. #14 of *101 of the Best Corporate Team-Building Activities*, 2nd ed. (Tacoma, WA: Tarrak Technologies, 2000). http://www.tarrak.com/BOOKS/101.htm

by making the bottom layer the infrastructure that they had to move first and composing the top layer of items that they could move or install only after everything else. Creating these categories allowed the team to multitask more efficiently, move critical items first, and complete the project in less than 50 percent of the previously estimated time! An added benefit came from using Google Docs to collaboratively create, update, and monitor status. This allowed every teammate to see what was happening in real time and enhanced team morale because they could see how quickly and efficiently they conducted the move. The team was even rewarded with an outing by the chief executive officer (CEO).

Project Matrix—Balance Time, Quality, and Performance to Complete a Project

Time: 30–60 minutes

Participants: 5–20 per team; unlimited teams

Technology: Internet, Google Docs or another application that allows simultaneous editing

Category: Problem solving

Goals

Increase team problem-solving skills such as time management, strategy, and tactics through a team taking turns navigating a hidden route through a 10 × 10 grid.

Game Summary

Project Matrix is based on a classic team-building event called Gridlock created by social scientist Rocky Kimball. Team members take turns trying to discover a hidden route through a 10 × 10 grid. This initiative is good for encouraging people to pay attention and solve problems as a group, allowing mistakes during the process, and completing it efficiently.

Setup

Log in to Google Docs. Leaving one column on the left and one column on the right, highlight a 10 × 10 grid and click Borders on the toolbar to create a grid on the playing area.

Share the document with your teammates by clicking the Share button (🔒 Share) and then typing all of your teammates' e-mail addresses. Set up a teleconference if your team is remote. Be sure to either print the solution sheet or post it on another part of your screen. Finally, have a stopwatch available.

Instructions to the Audience

(Call into telecom.) Open the document called Project Matrix, and you'll see yourself and your teammates represented as a box. Line up on the left side of the screen, outside of the grid. Your goal is to get from one side of the matrix to the other in the least amount of time and by taking the fewest number of incorrect steps. You'll take turns and have one person on the grid at a time. If you move and are on the path, there will be no noise. However, if you're off the path, you will get buzzed and will have to get back in line on the left-hand side. The mistake is a valuable learning opportunity, so you'll incur no penalties. However, every subsequent mistake will cost you a 1-minute penalty. You can only move up, down, left, or right. I'll give you 2 minutes to get into order and plan, and then the timer will begin.

(Make sure that as the facilitator, you have the solution in front of you so that you can buzz the team when they walk of the path. You can also cut and paste the red penalty square to mark when a team goes off the path, then add 1 minute to the penalty if they hit that square again. Make a note of the time when they exit on the right-hand side.)

Power Tips

You can reduce or increase the size of the grid to decrease or increase complexity.

You can require the group *not* to talk to increase the level of difficulty.

You can prohibit the group from modifying the grid to make the exercise harder (*or* you can reward teams if they do mark the grid as a way to avoid mistakes).

You can add dead ends (paths that do not lead to the end) or allow diagonal moves to increase difficulty.

I often make time marks on my sheet such as "3:45 team goes too slow to avoid mistakes" on the solution sheet to give me talking points for the debrief.

Debrief

What was your team's initial strategy? Who took what roles to support the entire team? What was fluid and what was frustrating? Did some people move too slow or too fast? How did your team feel about mistakes? How many repeated mistakes did your team make? What was the team dynamic like?

Case Study[3]

I first used Project Matrix with a struggling team with the goal of identifying four initiatives to help them. Project Matrix was sequenced to be first for the explicit reason that the team needed to be diagnosed. It was predicted in this case that the team would have trouble completing the task. Although team members thought of themselves as a high-functioning group, their manager did not; so this initiative would let them know whose assessment was correct.

This team was hesitant to make any mistakes initially, so they moved very slowly. Some members failed to pay attention to what was going on, resulting in multiple team members racking up penalties by stepping on the wrong square more than once. In the end, the team was pretty depressed; one member even remarked, "This is exactly what happens at work."

However, what I found useful as a designer and facilitator came when I then stacked three initiatives behind this one. The first covered one skill and was relatively easy; the second was a bit more challenging; and the third was fairly difficult. This momentum prompted the team to learn the key skill of team problem solving, use it to create success on the next team-building game, and use that momentum to complete each subsequent challenge in record times. This allowed the team to end on a high note, with all members making a strong commitment to one another to change how they work. They realized together that they'd much rather experience collective success than work hard individually only to fail as a team.

Chat Survivor—Setting Team Priorities and Making Hard Decisions

Time: 30–60 minutes

Participants: 2–8 per team; unlimited teams

Technology: BuddyMeeting or another online collaboration tool that can share slides and has chat features

Category: Problem solving, prioritization and decision making, consensus

Goals

Improve team problem-solving skills by assessing survival items, prioritizing through debate, and coming to consensus on the top five items to take for survival.

Game Summary

Chat Survivor is a tested simulation that teams and individuals use for survival training that has been converted online for shared presentations, teleconferences, or chat windows. It's a

---

[3]*Sources: Priest, S. #81 of 100 of the Best Virtual Team-Building Events.* (Seattle, WA: Tarrak Technologies, 2001). virtualteamworks.com; http://www.tarrak.com/BOOKS/100.htm

Priest, S. & Rohnke, K. #73 of *101 of the Best Corporate Team-Building Activities*, 2nd ed. (Tacoma, WA: Tarrak Technologies, 2000). http://www.tarrak.com/BOOKS/101.htm

great game to use to learn how your team establishes priorities and comes to group decisions. In addition, it shows how well your team can make decisions using a low-bandwidth medium such as chat.

Setup

Establish a teleconference number and PIN number. Log in to BuddyMeeting.com, start a new meeting, and fill in the information. Click Create. Copy the information and send it to all participants with the link to http://buddymeeting.com/join.php; include the date and time to log in. Log in to the meeting 15 to 30 minutes before the start time and click Start Meeting.

1. Click 📷 to Upload a document for presentation.
2. Click ⊙ to browse files.
3. Choose the Chat Survivor.pptx PowerPoint file in the BuddyMeeting folder of online resources or download from http://geoteaming.com/uploads/ChatSurvival.pptx
4. Click Upload:

Make sure you can see all the information on your slideshow. Go to slide 1, call into the teleconference line, and you're ready.

Instructions to the Audience

You and your teammates have just survived a small airplane crash. Take the time to read the scenario; then, by using *only* chat, decide on the *top* five items that your team will take from the plane. We will rank your choices at the end. We will begin a timer (default 10 minutes) and remember—*no talking* during this time.

Facilitator Notes

It can be helpful to give participants reminders at the 5-, 3-, and 1-minute mark to let them know how much time is left.

The chat log is extremely useful in highlighting specific points of team inflection during the debrief. In addition, you can right-click, select Copy All Text, and use it in post-processing or while writing a more in-depth study of team behaviors.

Debrief

What happened? How did you choose your five items? What did you learn from the process? Was the final decision unanimous or not? Who was the leader? Who had a decision-changing idea? How did you convince others to agree with your point of view? What can you take forward in your team meetings to make better decisions?

Case Study

The American Society for Training and Development ran Chat Survivor at their 2011 International Conference. Although participants were face to face, they could communicate to each other only over Twitter using specific hashtags during the 10-minute exercise; they then submitted their final answers to a shared hashtag. We received fascinating feedback from the 20+ teams. Some claimed that it was very challenging to keep track and create consensus using only text. Others found it highly engaging and told us that they came to a consensus very quickly, as they were all in agreement over the major items. Most believed that choosing the fourth and fifth items was the hardest part. The results produced scores that ranged from numbers in the 40s all the way to a team that had 16 (one away from the best score possible; lower scores are better in this event). Most of all, these training professionals experienced the same team dynamics they have with face-to-face team building online, and it opened many doors of possibilities that they hadn't ever considered.

CHAPTER

6

Creativity and Innovation

An essential aspect of creativity is not being afraid to fail.

—Edwin Land

Business is difficult. But it could be approached two ways: Seriously, or with the same way you're doing your job, with entertainment aspect, with pleasure, with fun. And we decided to try to make it as fun that we do our creativity.

—Guy Laliberté, creator of Cirque du Soleil

Teams use creativity to do much more than just solve problems. They tap into this resource to generate new products, services, and solutions that many didn't even realize they needed. For instance, the advent of the iPhone came as the consequence of the fact that people wanted a better phone that did more for them. This desire for improvement resulted in the wildly successful App Store, which did more than simply bring a new product into consumers' lives: It changed the culture and the very way that people used their phones. The app market hadn't even existed prior to this; but thanks to creativity, an entirely new consumer space was created—one that is now supported by thousands of developers and millions of users.

These team-building games focus on the process of creating something out of nothing. They encourage team members to generate new ideas and show them how to take a few simple goals and rules and hopefully produce magic. These games help hone the skills of improvisation, building on other people's ideas and coming up with new ways of thinking that can result in amazing solutions.

Twaiku—Twitter Poetry in Motion

Time: 10–20 minutes
Participants: 1–1,000
Technology: Twitter, text, chat, teleconference (optional)
Category: Creativity

Goals

Learn how to express creativity with limited resources from multiple people as your team produces a haiku (a Japanese-style poem) in 140 characters or less.

Game Summary

This quick Twitter, text, or chat initiative provides a tool that any team can use for enhancing creativity or reflecting on a previous team-building game by using a format that inspires beauty through brief, intense expression.

Setup

Arrange a unique hashtag on Twitter or use an existing hashtag, such as a conference hashtag (e.g., #astd12). You can also use text, chat, e-mail, or other ways of sending your teams' haiku. Input your slide deck with the question or topic that you're arranging. You can also use free online tools such as HootSuite Archives for archiving all of your results to share with your audience after the presentation.

Instructions to the Audience

A twaiku is a haiku posted on Twitter and therefore limited to 140 characters. Many of you know that a haiku is a poem that consists of three lines. The first line has five syllables, the second has seven, and the third line returns to five. You and your team need to work together and post a twaiku on the chosen topic within 5 minutes.

Suggested Topics for Twaikus

Secrets of teamwork, what you learned from this session, how you feel about this team, leadership tips, management challenges, solutions to a team challenge.

Power Tips

Use HootSuite Archives to save an archive of all the twaikus for future reference.

Debrief

Take the time to read through the results and recognize the people who contributed. If possible, interview the authors and find out how they collaborated as a team. You can also ask what others thought about the contributor's twaiku. If you're working in a trusting environment, you might ask others to vote on the best twaiku and ask what made it the best.

Case Study[1]

Atyourlibrary.org ran a contest in April 2011 for Twaikus about libraries. They were overwhelmed by the more than 250 responses they received! As a result, they generated a lot of awareness about people's perception of the value of libraries. In the final voting @classic sixbooks won with this entry, receiving 28 percent of the votes:

> *from books to gaming/yes, the best in life is free/at your library*
>   *Here were the top four runner-ups:*
> 1. It is known as the/People's University/life-long learners here. @TinaPlatt
> 2. Last year I paid naught/And kept a count as I read/Two hundred plus books @dakiMel
> 3. Land Of Endless Dreams/Here Nothing Is As It Seems/High School Library @BlondieTaughtMe
> 4. With toddler at home/Grad study is not easy/Saved by library @PavlikM
>   *As you can see there is a hidden depth in this simple format that can really communicate strongly with brevity.*

> Twaiku fan page with definition: http://twitter.pbworks.com/w/page/1779937/Twaiku-(haiku-written-in-twitter)

> Great examples of twaikus: http://haitotheku.com/

One Text at a Time Expert—Team Answers One Text at a Time

Time: 5–20 minutes

Participants: 2–6 per team; multiple teams

Technology: Text, chat, TweetChat, Google Docs

Category: Creativity

---

[1]*Source:* atyourlibrary.org. Used with permission.

Goals

Learn team creativity by listening to each other, reacting in the moment to build on another teammate's idea, and going with the team flow by answering a question as an expert, texting one word at a time.

Game Summary

Text at a Time encourages active listening, being in the moment, relinquishing control, and working as a team. You'll know when you create flow because funny or enlightening answers will emerge. It will be obvious when the flow is missing as well; people won't listen and will not be able to make sense or play off of each other's ideas.

Setup

Create four to six questions that you can ask this team of experts. You can start with easy topics, such as "How are you?" and work your way to more technical topics, such as "How should we handle this client?" Make sure you have everybody's cell phone number if you're calling in. If you're using online chat, start a conversation for each team or have each person log into a website like BuddyMeeting.com. Another option is to use Google Docs so that team members can edit the document simultaneously.

Instructions to the Audience

(These instructions assume you have four people per team. You can change this number from two to six.) Number yourselves from one to four. The four people in each group have been tasked to become *one* expert. I will ask you a series of questions. Person number 1 will go first and text or chat one word. Then each subsequent member of the group will continue. Continue cycling through each team member (in order from person 1 to person 4) until you have the answer to the question. To signify the answer is complete, type "period." Remember: Since you are *experts*, you *must* know the answer.

Debrief

Is the expert (the team answering the question) in flow or out of flow? Are you listening actively and replying spontaneously? Are you able to let go of your preconceived ideas and build on what people are saying? What can you do to support your team's result and improve your expert answer?

Variations

Have participants do the following one text at a time:

Text at a Time Story: Tell a story.

Text at a Time Movie: Describe a movie.

Text at a Time Training: Create a training lesson.

Text at a Time Letters: Write a letter. If two or more teams are participating, one team can respond to the other's letter. (A good topic here might be customer service letters.)

Text at a Time Adventure: Create an adventure.

Section at a Time Story with Twitter Feeds: @janicefryatt is an improvisational facilitator who was asked to lead a team-building initiative for Event Camp Europe. She had four people tell a story live. One person would start, and she'd point to another person to pick up where the last person left off. Web communications company Sonic Foundry streamed the event live, which allowed people to watch and send information via Twitter that they wanted to incorporate into the story. The result was a hilarious story that engaged both live and virtual audiences.

Case Study

We once worked with a team that was notorious for talking over one another, starting side conversations, and wondering why they weren't on the same page during face-to-face conversations. Of course, these tendencies carried over into their online communication. Team members failed to read and reply to critical e-mails, while others went off on tangents when all that had been requested was a simple yes or no.

We used Text at a Time Expert as an opening to their digital team-building session. Initially, we had to coach the team members to not text out of turn. The paradox of improvisation is that people think you need to be spontaneous and have chaos; however, Text at a Time adds structure to creativity. Once this group began to habitually listen to and wait for one another, they started producing some fast *and* hilarious answers. Combined with a collection of three other team-building initiatives, this exercise elicited feedback that this team was ready for change. This initiative put them in the mind-set to achieve breakthroughs in team process.

WWMTD?—What Would My Team Do If They Had to Make a Creative License Plate?

Time: 10–30 minutes

Participants: 2–6 per team; multiple teams

Technology: Internet browser

Category: Creativity

Goals

Use team creativity and innovation to create slogans from letters and numbers in the format of a vanity license plate.

Game Summary

WWMTD is a fast, easy game that sparks creativity and has the added bonus of producing the winning team's slogan into an actual license plate in a cost-effective manner.

Setup

Send a link to www.buildasign.com/LicensePlates to each team and make sure they have it open when the team-building activity starts. If you're holding the game remotely, set up a BuddyMeeting.com meeting and send the appropriate information to each team. One lead in each team will share his or her screen with the license plate displayed so that everyone can see the design being worked on. In addition, arrange for one central BuddyMeeting for people to log in to once they are done working. Set up a single e-mail address to which each team should send its finished license plate. Be ready to upload the designs into Buddy-Meeting.com so that all participants can review them. Finally, set up a telecom if you're holding the meeting remotely.

Instructions to Audience

You will have 8 minutes to create a license plate with a meaning that represents a team slogan. When you are done, save your license plate and send it to me. We'll all hang up from the individual BuddyMeeting and log in to a central BuddyMeeting, where we'll see all the teams' designs.

Debrief

How did your team decide on the words you used? Did you allow filler words like *a, the, in,* and *of* in between major letters, or did you strictly adhere to the letters given to you? What words did you suggest but not use? Why? How collaborative was your effort? How can you apply what you learned to your work?

Variations

Have all teams use the same license plate.

Have teams precreate license plates that another team has to use.

Specify other themes.

Allow the team to change one letter on the license plate.

Come up with a license plate on the spot so that no one has an advantage.

Case Study

During one of our team building events, teams generated the following license plates:

RSBPPL = ReSponsiBility needs Practice, Patience, and Love
HBGLTR = Having Big Goals makes us Leverage Team Resources
WODNMSS = Working Overtime Doesn't Necessarily Mean Sure Success

You can look online for some great ideas for using combinations of letters and numbers, such as this *Star Wars*–inspired license plate: MYD4SBWU = May(MY) the(D) force(4S) be (B) with(W) you(U).

Team Pictionary—Communicating through Drawing

Time: 10–45 minutes
Participants: 2–6 per team; multiple teams
Technology: Whiteboard, Google Docs
Category: Creativity

Goals

Increase your team's creativity and rapport by having your team correctly guess what your teammate is drawing on an online whiteboard. This team-building game also increases a team's ability to use the drawing functions of an online whiteboard.

Game Summary

This exercise posts the classic game of Pictionary online. Team members will begin to learn the various tools that each online whiteboard provides and get a feel for drawing with a mouse or other input device.

Setup

Come up with at least 15 words that are related to your field of work or your individual team. Then set up an online Web conference using a service such as BuddyMeeting.com and invite the other members.

1. Click  to upload your document for presentation.

2. Click ⊙ to browse files.

3. Choose ▤ **Blank Presentation** and select the PowerPoint file in the Buddy-Meeting folder of online resources or download the blank PowerPoint file from http://www.geoteaming.com/uploads/Blank.pptx.

4. Click Upload:

5. Click the ⊡ in the chat window.

6. Select all the people to chat with privately and a new tab for each person will appear:

Set a timer—either one on your computer, your phone, or a stopwatch—for 60 seconds. Finally, set up a teleconference line to explain and debrief the game.

Instructions to the Audience

During this Team Pictionary game, you will select one of your teammates to draw using the online whiteboard. Other members of the team must then guess what that teammate is drawing. You will have 60 seconds to guess. The person drawing cannot talk or use letters or numbers in the drawing. We will alternate teams, and the team with the most correct answers wins.

Chat privately with the person selected from the first team and send him or her the first word or phrase:

Switch the presenter to that person:

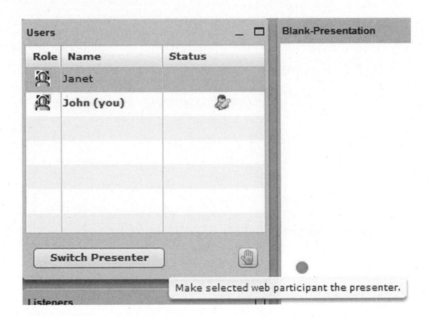

Have them click (the Show Whiteboard button) and make sure they know how to draw by holding down the mouse button and clicking the red X () to clear the whiteboard.

When you say "go," start the timer and give the person drawing 60 seconds to have his or her team guess what is being drawn.

Keep score and announce a winner after 14 questions have been completed; or, use the 15th question as a tiebreaker. You can use fewer or more questions to control the time for this event.

Power Tips

You can designate some words as All Play words, meaning that one person draws and every team can guess. Using multiperson drawing programs such as Google Docs, every team could draw at the same time.

Debrief

Who is the best drawer and why? What communication shortcuts did your team learn? What new online whiteboard tools did you learn? To what projects and assignments can you apply this new tool at work?

Case Study[2]

Team Pictionary was used with teams that routinely had to draw room setups with their clients and transmit them to the operations team. This group then had to input the sketches into a professional drawing program and send it back to the client. They also used this

---

[2]*Sources:* Priest, S. #18 of *100 of the Best Virtual Team-Building Events*. (Seattle, WA: Tarrak Technologies, 2001). virtualteamworks.com; http://www.tarrak.com/BOOKS/100.htm
Priest, S., Sikes, S. & Evans, F. #89 of *99 of the Best Experiential Corporate Games We Know*. (Lakebay, WA: eXperientia, 2000). http://www.tarrak.com/BOOKS/99.htm

information when setting up the room—so any miscommunication meant a lot of extra, unnecessary work, which subsequently burnt out an already overworked staff.

After completing this basic assignment, the sales and operation teams created initiatives based on real client needs (such as 10 rounds of 8 with a stage, podium, projectors on both sides, and four rectangular tables in the back). They began to generate ideas for shortcuts by using the shapes and numbers and doing it in real time so that remote sales teams could work with operations to figure out what was and was not possible or advisable. They soon had systems that allowed the salespeople to interact live with operations while working with clients. Using their shortcuts allowed them to draft a plan that an operations person could use immediately after completing the call. The clients were impressed with the high level of teamwork and use of technology. The operations teams increased their accuracy in giving the client what they wanted and reduced their resets by more than 20 percent in the following months. In addition, the sales team was able to sell 10 percent more because they didn't spend any dead time after the client meeting recreating work and submitting it to the operations team. A simple game turned into a significant competitive advantage when everyone—literally everyone—got on the same page.

Mind Mapping—Visual Brainstorming for Teams

Time: 10–60 minutes

Participants: 2–12 per team; infinite teams

Technology: Internet browser

Goals

Increase team creativity, innovation, and strategic planning and problem-solving capabilities by using an accelerated learning technique known as mind mapping.

Game Summary

Tony Buzan created Mind Mapping to serve as an upgrade for note-taking. By designing a tree-like diagram, you can quickly see relationships and the overview of all the data. Team Mind Mapping allows groups to work on their various areas of focus and come up with solutions that are triggered by other people's ideas, thereby increasing overall collaboration.

Setup

1. Go to http://mindmeister.com.
2. Click Sign Up For Free:

Sign Up For Free

3. Click Basic:

4. Enter your info (or use a Gmail account or Facebook to log in, which is what I did):

5. Click New Mind Map:

6. Click Share:

Then enter all the teammates' e-mail addresses. They will receive an invite with instructions for creating a new account or login.

Instructions to the Audience

Your team will have 10 minutes to brainstorm on the topic we have. To enter a new idea, click on an area and then press the Insert key and a new node will appear. At the end of the 10 minutes, we'll review all of the ideas and see if we can make a decision.

Power Tips

Mind Mapping has been used for planning, process improvement, scheduling, and project management, among many other uses. Power tips include the ability to drag and drop pictures, URLs, documents, and many other types of information into the map.

Debrief

Who created the most nodes? Who created the fewest? Did other people's nodes spark new ideas for you? If so, which ones? What is helpful—and challenging—about seeing everyone's input this way? Do you think we made a better or worse team decision this way? Why?

Case Study

Judith Glaser, chief executive officer (CEO) of Benchmark Communications, Inc., was asked to review an early copy of Tony Buzan's book on Mind Mapping. Judith was the ideal candidate for this, as someone whose mind was always going in a million directions at once. Mind Mapping allowed her to think analytically *and* creatively at the same time while capturing and organizing the many thoughts that crossed her mind. Judith used Mind Mapping with the teams she worked with as a key technique for moving from *I* (or *my* idea) to *we* (or *our* ideas combined). By working on the Mind Map together, she formed a bond and a trust with her clients as they cocreated the solutions they needed. Judith even cites the value of Mind Mapping in terms of body chemistry: The brain releases oxytocin when teams feel connected. She has done research on how Mind Mapping helps teams release oxytocin to quell fear and increase bonding between teammates, leading to financial and conceptual success.

Link to entire article authored by Judith E. Glaser written for womenentrepreneur.com: http://www.foxbusiness.com/personal-finance/2011/01/05/mind-mapping-new-way-think/

YouTeams—iMovie-Based Team Building

Time: 1–4 hours
Participants: 2–200; up to 8 per team
Technology: iPad 2, iMovie
Category: Creativity

Goals

Build team creativity and innovation while learning the technical skills of writing, directing, editing, and uploading a movie.

Game Summary

Although moviemaking has been around for a while and can serve as an effective team-building event, it historically required at least a camera, a laptop, download cables, and expensive software. The iPad 2 revolutionized this by placing camera, video, and editor in one thin package that is very easy to learn.

Setup

Acquire one iPad 2 for each team and install iMovie ($4.99 from the App Store) on each. If your company or team does not own iPad 2's, you can rent them for your event from an AV company such as www.psav.com. You can also print out the roles sheet http://tinyurl.com/youteams to help with instructions and provide a pad of Post-its to help with storyboarding, a brainstorming technique that helps move the production process along.

Instructions to the Audience

Each team has an iPad 2. Play the iPad 2 iMovie Guided Tour at http://www.apple.com/ipad/guided-tours/. (Wait for teams to watch the tour.) Each group's assignment is to write, film, edit, and upload a video on a chosen topic. We have given you suggested roles and materials to storyboard your concept until you're ready to film. Most teams start with the main goal and then storyboard the idea while assigning roles and collecting the videos and photos they need; then they finish assembling before time expires. If you need any help, you can touch

"My Projects": and touch the question-mark icon () on the bottom left to get Help. Touch the camera icon (📷) on the right side of the screen to shoot pictures or videos for your movie. Then touch the Video, Photo, or Note icon to view your created videos, photos, and music:

Tap the download arrow to add your shots into your timeline:

Try tapping or double-tapping each item to edit and add titles:

When you're done, tap My Projects:

and then the upload key at the bottom of the screen (just to the right of the play button):

Here is the username and password of the account that we'll all be uploading to. (Insert YouTube username or password here.)

Suggested Topics

Secrets of teamwork

What did you learn from this session?

How do you feel about this team?

Leadership tips, management challenges, solutions to a team challenge

Film your team as a trailer to a movie

Film in the style of a news report

Power Tips

The uploading of the video from the iPad2 can sometimes be a time-consuming process, so test your Internet connection with a 3 min or so movie and time how long it takes to process and upload your video. If it takes more than 5 minutes, then remove uploading the video from this game and just play the video direct from iMovie on the iPad2 and then upload the videos after the game is over.

Because you can share these videos easily, you gain extended value from this event by assembling a learning video that other teams can access at any time in the future, thereby building a library of content generated by employees instead of trainers. Participants will also develop the very valuable skills needed to create a video, from overcoming technical obstacles to figuring out artistic challenges. These skills are increasingly sought after and necessary for employees to exhibit in order for them to have an impact on their organizations.

In addition, view any video with more than 1 million hits and search for articles about videos that go viral to give the team key lessons on how to make successful videos. And if you can't afford iPads, you can do One Take Movies with a digital camera and have people shoot the movie in one continuous shot or use the free Windows Live Essentials: Movie Maker with a PC that has a camera.

Debrief

After the teams have completed the team-building game and their movie, create a Movie Night by having popcorn for all the finished teams. Have a connection to a projector and a set of speakers. You can use one computer to stream the movies online, or you can buy the video connector (VGA or HDMI) for the iPad 2 and play them directly from each iPad. Ask each team to give a small director's cut commentary; then show the movie and solicit audience feedback. Most of these will be extremely funny, and you'll see great flashes of creativity. You can also have teams vote for the best video (they can't vote for their own team); remember to ask for comments on what made it the best.

Case Study

At one team-building event, we had teams create videos about bringing one of the company's values, "financial," to life. They produced a video with the key concept of getting three quotes for any purchase they were going to make. A random insert of a hilarious mask at the 0:59 mark made everyone laugh at the video. When I polled people at the end, more than 90 percent were able to remember the key message: getting three quotes! This is a sure way to encourage fun and effective team building and training in the world of viral videos.

Get three quotes: http://www.youtube.com/watch?v=fZO2RkJNEZs

What happens when pros use iPad 2 and iMovie: http://news.cnet.com/8301-30685_3-20042669-264.html

2011 report on statistics on videos that go viral: http://mashable.com/2011/01/26/viral-videos-infographic/

YouTeams Planning Sheet: http://tinyurl.com/youteams

GooseChase—Cell Phone Photo Scavenger Hunt

Time: 30–120 minutes

Participants: 2–1,000; free for 4 teams

Technology: GooseChase on iOS, Droid, and BlackBerry phones (more to be added)

Category: Creativity

Goals

Discover team creativity while increasing team cooperation, strategy, and innovation by participating in a cell phone photo scavenger hunt.

Game Summary

GooseChase is a great app from the genius minds at Waterloo, Canada. The basic idea is to take the simple and effective photo scavenger hunt and make it all work from a cell phone. This initiative sparks teamwide creativity and strategy while building a strong online community—with the bonus of getting to master your cell phone's camera.

Setup

The planner must login to http://goosechase.com and create a mission list. Then each team needs to download GooseChase onto at least one phone per team.

Instructions to the Audience

This is a cell phone photo scavenger hunt, so each team will receive a hunt number and a password that will unlock all the missions. Your team's job is to complete as many missions as possible and score the most points before the time expires. If you're late, you will lose 10 percent of your points for every minute you're late.

Power Tips

Adding Hail Mary challenges that allow teams who are behind to catch up can help them complete very complex or challenging team missions.

GooseChase can be done entirely indoors or around the world in virtual locations. You can even do both simultaneously if you make your challenges generic enough to be completed anywhere in the world.

Debrief

What was your team's strategy? What actually happened in the field? What creativity did you discover about your team? Who do you know better from participating in this event? What will you do different with your team now?

Case Study

We ran this event with a collection of high-level CXOs such as CEOs, CFOs, etc. from a company. The twist was that we added a Hail Mary mission of getting your back waxed for about four times the points of the highest mission. Out of seven teams, *six* chose to get their backs waxed and took photos of it. It's a pretty safe bet that none of these participants will forget this team-building event, especially the six who endured this "beauty" treatment—something that exhibits a critical lesson: You'll do more for your team than you'll ever do for yourself.

Team GarageBand—Build a Song, Build a Team

Time: 60–120 minutes
Participants: 2–12 per team

Technology: iPad 2, GarageBand app
Category: Creativity

Goals

Highlight team creativity, song writing ability, music composition, instrument performance, and vocal talents while your teams compete to write the best song on a specific theme in the time allotted.

Game Summary

GarageBand is a $4.99 app that you can buy for an iPad 2. This app provides an entire production studio that teams can utilize to create a full-fledged song. Anyone can make a song with Smart Instruments, samples, and multitrack recording, even those with *no* musical talent. The resulting teamwork is usually hilarious and shows you how much people can do when they're put to the challenge.

Setup

Make sure each team has one iPad 2 and buy the GarageBand app. Create the message of the song or keywords the song must include.

Instructions to the Audience

Your team will have a total of 45 minutes to write, produce, and publish an award-winning song on the chosen topic. You will take a short video tour of GarageBand; then you will need to write lyrics, lay down a drum track, put instruments over it, and finally, add your lyrics to the song before time is up.

Power Tips

Doing a parody of an existing song can really help a team move fast to create a high-quality and funny production. You can find all the lyrics and the song online and then attempt to mimic the key components.

Another fast way of creating a song is using all the Smart Instruments on GarageBand, as they will do all the arranging for you. Finally, you can also use the loops that are built into the app; layering over loops allows you to generate your original song track and really focus on the lyrics and singing.

Debrief

Who took what role? How did you decide on the song structure? What hidden talents did you discover within your team members? What technology did you use to enhance your team talent? What did you learn that you can use moving forward in professional situations?

Case Study

I knew that I had to try this myself, so I looked for what was a very popular song at the time, "Party Rock Anthem." I found the lyrics online and the YouTube video (with more than 372 million hits at that point!). I copied the lyrics into OneNote and started editing them. Then, by playing the YouTube video and searching "Party Rock Anthem GarageBand," I was able to find the key components of the song from other people who covered it. I laid down each track and copied and pasted it as much as possible.

Although writing the lyrics is definitely the most challenging part, it's also the most rewarding for the team member who takes the risk of putting his or her voice on the song. This relates very closely to the kind of things that tend to happen at work—situations where salespeople take the lead or customer service people become the voice of the company.

I came up with this result in less than 60 minutes: http://www.youtube.com/watch?v=IJNjtAL3O-E. Although I need some serious auto-tuning, I think it's respectable for an hour's worth of work.

There are also entire companies, such as http://songdivision.com, devoted to producing live songs as team-building exercises; these companies bring in professional musicians and more, and they can help create catchy songs that can become a company anthem for the next year!

CHAPTER 7

Collaboration

Unity is strength . . . when there is teamwork and collaboration, wonderful things can be achieved.

— Mattie Stepanek

Collaboration is the key to unlocking a team's potential. By learning how to work together, you can achieve those mythical results that are more than the sum of the parts. The digital team-building games in this chapter address situations in which two or more teams come together and show how multiple teams can collaborate to create effective and lasting results. Perhaps the most inspiring story is one where 50 people collaborated in just 90 minutes to create an entire case study that might have taken months for an individual to finish—a task that boasted solutions that incorporated experiences from 50 different experts. Now *that's* value.

Office Move—Working Together to Switch Places

Time: 20–30 minutes
Participants: 6–12, even numbers
Technology: Google Docs
Category: Collaboration

Goals

Increase collaboration between two teams as they attempt to change places by taking turns to move according to a set of rules.

Game Summary

This is a classic team-building event called Traffic Jam that originally came from Karl Rohnke's *Silver Bullets* that has been updated to an online environment. This event encourages the collaboration that comes about when two groups work together to solve problems by implementing inclusion and planning. It's a classic because it brings out team-building issues in a short amount of time for teams that are unaware of the solution.

Setup

Create a Google Doc spreadsheet. Set it up according to the diagram and click the Share button to share the document with all the teammates:

You can conduct this event live or arrange a teleconference for all teammates if you're doing it virtually.

	A	B	C	D	E	F	G	H	I	J	K	L
Office Move												
Start	A	B	C	D	E			1	2	3	4	5
Current	A	B	C	D	E			1	2	3	4	5
End		1	2	3	4	5	A	B	C	D	E	
Rules												
	1 You can only move forward											
	2 You must remain on a space											
	3 You can only move into open spaces											
	4 You can only move around a person from the opposite side into the next open space											
	5 You can only move around one person at a time											
	6 Only one person may move at a time											
	Use Ctrl-X and Ctrl-V to move											

Instructions to the Audience

It's time for an office move where the team on the left side needs to exchange places with those on the right side. There are six rules that you cannot break; if you do, you'll need to start over. You have only 10 attempts before you waste so much time that you'll be "fired." The rules are:

1. You can move forward only.
2. You must remain on a space.
3. You can move into open spaces only.
4. You can move around a person only from the opposite side into the next open space.
5. You can move around only one person at a time.
6. Only one person may move at a time.

An easy way to move is to put your cursor on the location you want to move from, hit Ctrl+X (to cut; Command+X on a Mac), move to your new location and hit Ctrl+V (to paste; Command+V on a Mac). Are there any questions? Then begin!

Debrief

Look to see if the group plans and creates a joint strategy or if they just begin moving without asking questions of one another or discussing anything. A key point is to determine whether a team is too eager and begins moving prematurely, blocking the entire process. On the other side, the teams can become trapped in "analysis paralysis" if they talk so long that they *never* start moving—and therefore never solve the challenge. Reaching your internal time limit is a good indication that you need to call a time-out and discuss what is going on with your team before continuing.

Another interesting discussion can emerge if you observe a team making an illegal move and don't say anything. Do the teams police themselves, or does everyone just ignore when teams do things they aren't supposed to? This kind of question can incite excellent valuable conversation about compliance, ethics, and integrity that team members can consider in light of real-world consequences for breaking the rules.

Finally, look for team momentum to build as people recognize the pattern and begin to move quickly because of it. The trick to finding and remembering a solution lies in this hint: Once a side begins to move, everyone on that side moves unless a move puts one person behind another person from the other side (avoid this situation since it makes a two-person block against the other side and you'll have to start over). The following figure shows the key steps to the 35-step solution for 10 people.

Move											
Begin	A	B	C	D	E		1	2	3	4	5
1	A	B	C	D	E	1		2	3	4	5
2–3	A	B	C		D	1	E	2	3	4	5
4–6	A	B	C	1	D	2	E	3		4	5
7–10	A		B	1	C	2	D	3	E	4	5
11–15	A	1	B	2	C	3	D	4	E	5	
16–20		1	A	2	B	3	C	4	D	5	E
21–25	1	2	A	3	B	4	C	5	D		E
26–29	1	2		3	A	4	B	5	C	D	E
30–32	1	2	3	4	A	5	B		C	D	E
33–34	1	2	3	4		5	A	B	C	D	E
35	1	2	3	4	5		A	B	C	D	E

Case Study[1]

Two virtual teams that work together—one that's located here in the United States and another development group in India—completed the Office Move game by connecting via teleconference and the Internet. The one thing that everyone noticed immediately was that everybody on each team seemed to be talking at once; nobody understood anything because the teleconference line cut out when two or more people spoke simultaneously. Finally, a teammate from India suggested that they follow a protocol that only one person speak at a time. The groups spent 15 minutes talking over the ideas but not moving at all. They eventually arrived at the strategy to the solution, and both parties agreed to attempt it.

Then they started moving. This was the first time I had seen a team complete the task successfully on their first attempt. They communicated a great deal before someone made a move; the process moved increasingly faster as each teammate bought into the plan and

[1]*Sources:* Priest, S. #67 of *100 of the Best Virtual Team-Building Events.* (Seattle, WA: Tarrak Technologies, 2001). virtualteamworks.com; http://www.tarrak.com/BOOKS/100.htm

Priest, S. & Rohnke, K. #7 of *101 of the Best Corporate Team-Building Activities,* 2nd ed. (Tacoma, WA: Tarrak Technologies, 2000). http://www.tarrak.com/BOOKS/101.htm

recognized the pattern. The final half of the moves took a mere 3 minutes to complete—and teams had switched places with no failed attempts!

During the debrief, the team members realized that the planning at the beginning paid off immensely. This led them to see that they had *not* been doing this at work. They had been working on code and then "throwing it over the wall" to the other team at the end of the workday. This created a great deal of work, rework, and frustration about doing it two different ways. The exercise led the employees to hold a meeting about defining goals and process. As a result, the team hit a key milestone ahead of schedule for the very first time!

Mergers and Reorgs—Getting Two Teams to Collaborate and Integrate Rapidly

Time: 20–30 minutes

Participants: 8–10; even numbers

Technology: Interactive whiteboard

Category: Collaboration

Goals

Increase collaboration between two teams and discover team styles, communication methods, and levels of trust as the two teams work to create an integrated team.

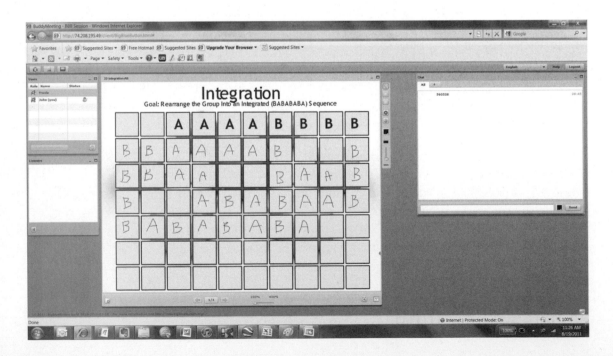

Game Summary

This is a classic team-building event called 2 × 4; it also originally came from Karl Rohnke's *Silver Bullets*. This activity focuses on problem solving, looking for issues with integration, observing how fellow team members act when merging, and figuring out how to work with new teammates.

Setup

Set up a meeting on BuddyMeeting.com or another Web conferencing service and invite participants. Download the graphic for this initiative from http://tinyurl.com/mergerandreorgs. Load the graphic for this initiative into BuddyMeeting.com. Have instructions ready to read and cut and paste into a chat window.

Instructions to the Audience

Your group represents two teams. Your task is to integrate these two teams in such a way that no one is standing beside anyone from the same team. Since change can be uncomfortable, no one will be asked to move on his or her own; instead, each person must do so accompanied by a partner. Therefore, we're moving pairs of adjacent people. As partners change, they cannot switch relative positions, and you can move only to unoccupied spaces. Any questions?

Power Tips

You can add individual ownership by allowing each person to draw only his or her own letter.

Debrief

The goal is to have the group increase performance until they can complete the task in four moves. Observe how the two teams work together (or fail to do so) in the beginning. Look for the key moment when someone from team A needs to work with and move with someone from team B and determine how that happened. Ask team members what has to happen for them to merge and work better together in a short amount of time. You could end up having each team request that the other somehow make the merger easier.

Case Study[2]

We ran this team-building event with two major companies (A and B) who had just signed a joint agreement. We divided the 80 people involved into 10 groups of eight. In each of

[2]*Sources:* Priest, S. #68 of *100 of the Best Virtual Team-Building Events*. (Seattle, WA: Tarrak Technologies, 2001). virtualteamworks.com; http://www.tarrak.com/BOOKS/100.htm

Priest, S. & Rohnke, K. #8 of *101 of the Best Corporate Team-Building Activities*, 2nd ed. (Tacoma, WA: Tarrak Technologies, 2000). http://www.tarrak.com/BOOKS/101.htm

the sessions, we had four team members from company A and four team members from company B who were going to work with one another in the same division—and who had met each other only briefly earlier in the day.

The teams initially began to work together but then ran into cultural conflicts. Company A was very entrepreneurial, whereas company B came from a more risk-averse corporate culture. Therefore, A wanted to move fast and make mistakes, whereas B wanted to slow the process and plan more before making any moves. They did agree to work on the solution on the teleconference and use the chat window to display their thoughts, since this approach was faster than drawing on the whiteboard. Team members started citing ideas rapidly, and eventually they figured out the entire solution in four lines of the chat window. They then worked together to fill in the main sheet with no mistakes.

The debrief highlighted the entrepreneurial team's willingness to experiment; they found an appropriate avenue for doing so in the chat window. It also gave the risk-averse team credit for planning the overall solution and being able to deliver the final product correctly the first time. Both teams made requests: Company A wanted to find safe places to experiment, and company B wanted to allocate time for overall strategy and planning to ensure they had a complete solution before they presented to the larger teams.

Broken Squares—Giving Is Better Than Getting for Team Collaboration

Time: 20–60 minutes

Participants: 5 per team; infinite teams

Technology: Internet, Google Docs, one computer per participant

Category: Collaboration

Goals

Increase team collaboration by learning the key lesson of giving to other team members as they work together to build five triangles.

Game Summary

This is a classic team-building event called Broken Squares that I posted online using Google Docs. The key lesson with this game is that the more you share, the faster you will achieve your goals. Conversely, you can hold up the entire team if you hoard your pieces or your solution.

Setup

Go to http://tinyurl.com/brokensquares. Then go to File > Make a copy:

Broken Squares ☆

File	Edit	View	Insert	Format	Arra

Share...

Publish to the Web...

See revision history

New   ►

Open...   Ctrl+O

Rename...

Make a copy...

Make a copy for yourself and enough copies for each team. Share the game with the five team members who are going to work together. Set up a teleconference line.

Instructions to the Audience

Please connect to the Google Doc Broken Squares document through the link I sent you. Let me know when all five of your teammates have arrived. (Wait for the team members to connect.) Each teammate will select an area for your three parts; there are three spots on the top and two on the bottom. Your goal is to put together five squares, one in front of each of you. Here are the rules:

1. You may use only the pieces provided.
2. No member may speak, gesture, or text another member throughout the activity.
3. Members may not ask another member for a piece, take a piece from another member, or signal in any way that another person is to give him or her a piece.
4. Members may give pieces to other members.
5. Members may not place their puzzle pieces in the center area for other team members to take.

Any questions? Okay, remember—no talking! *Go!*

Debrief

Your role here is part observer and part judge. You need to make sure that each participant is following the rules. It is okay for a member to give away all the pieces to his or her puzzle even if that person has already formed a square; in fact, it's usually a good sign for a team.

In addition, answer the following questions:

How willing were members to give away pieces of the puzzle *or* completed squares?

Did anyone finish his or her puzzle and then withdraw from the group problem-solving efforts? If so, how did it affect the rest of the team? This behavior is indicative of someone with a silo mentality who generally cares more about completing his or her own work than reaching the team goal. This mind-set can diminish the chances of finding a teamwide solution in this case, since an individual might be using a vital part of someone else's triangle.

Did dominant individuals emerge, or did everyone seem to participate equally and share leadership?

Did you see frustration emerging? If so, how? And how did it affect the group?

Case Study

An association board used the Broken Squares exercise at one of their retreats. In this case, there were three teams of five people each. Although the first team took a moment to get started, the team members completed a square and then gave the entire square to a teammate who was struggling. That teammate reciprocated by giving all the pieces to the person who was solving squares rapidly. This team accidentally created four squares out of the parts, but the facilitator clarified the goals to be five squares. So the team went back to working on the solution and completed five squares in just 4½ minutes. According to the facilitator, this was one of the *fastest* times to date. It came as a result of having the best people give away their work, while the slower individuals remained open to accepting help and giving their pieces away to others.

The second team completed in about 9 minutes, and the last team took more than 17 minutes to complete. While watching this table, the facilitator noticed that they felt more and more pressure about being late and having 10 other people observing them. In addition, people who had completed squares did *not* give their work to others. This meant that those having trouble were forced to figure it out on their own, and they were not making much progress. There were a variety of comments during the debrief, but the key lessons were to share when you or your group was ahead and to accept help when you were behind. This led to a more productive board retreat and, more important, prompted the group to alter its corporate environment. They encouraged people to seek help when they were behind in goals and guide others if they were ahead on projects. As a result, the board achieved many of its annual goals.

Team Timely.is—Collaborating a Month's Worth of Tweets and Updates

Time: 10–30 minutes
Participants: 2–90
Technology: Internet, Timely.is
Category: Collaboration

Goals

Increase team collaboration, communication, and marketing by creating a collection of tweets and updates together as a team.

Game Summary

This is a cool tool that James Spellos (@jspellos) showed me in one of his Hot Technology sessions. Timely.is is a website that evaluates the effectiveness of a company's last 200 tweets or Facebook status updates and schedules all upcoming tweets at times that will have the most significant effect. With 2 to 90 teammates logging in at once and sending one to five messages each, a team could fill an entire schedule of tweets while learning what everyone else is doing—and create their entire marketing plan for a month.

Setup

Go to Timely.is. Create an account with an e-mail and a password. Then connect the account to either your Twitter account or your Facebook account.

Instructions to the Audience

Please log into http://timely.is with the provided e-mail address and password. This website, called Timely.is, will schedule three tweets a day at optimal times by reviewing the previous 199 tweets. Let's brainstorm as a team and enter a total of 90 updates that our clients will love. You can post info, links, pictures, quotes, or anything you think will be a benefit to them. Afterward, we'll review what we have and see what we have learned from one another.

Debrief

Look for interesting trends in the messages. Allow all team members to read through the stream and then ask what they learned about things they didn't know were occurring. Ask how reading one post from someone sparked another post from someone else. If someone was stuck, what happened to get that person unstuck?

If you run this team-building game on a regular basis, then you click the Performance tab and look at the statistics for the last 199 tweets or updates and see which ones had the most impact including retweets, shares, clicks, and # of impressions made. A team can continually learn what works and do more of that style to get more reactions from people.

Case Study

A team used Team Timely.is as a quick way to update its clients on the process of what was going on behind the scenes at its organization and to create connections to the fans of the company by getting to know some of the teammates. Upon reviewing the stream, one teammate noticed that another teammate was working on a similar project. The two saw the overlap during the debrief and then met after the event to discuss the matter. They reported at the next team meeting that they were able to save 20 hours of development time by collaborating on the work they had each been completing individually!

Team Haiku—Write a Team Haiku/One Word at a Time Online

Time: 10–20 minutes
Participants: 2–5 per team
Technology: Google Docs
Category: Collaboration

Goals

Increase team collaboration and learn to use simultaneous editing tools as the team works together to create a haiku (or other type of poetry).

Game Summary

Small team-building initiatives like this can help a team learn the mechanics of simultaneous team document editing. In addition, the team can create humorous but valuable and memorable lessons for team building, leadership, or best practices.

Setup

Make sure each team member can access Google Docs or another simultaneous editing tool. Before the event, break the group into teams of two to six people and send the list of e-mail addresses around. Arrange a video or teleconference line for everyone to use during the activity.

Instructions to the Audience

The goal is for your team to create a haiku on the chosen topic in less than 5 minutes and then select one of your teammates to represent your team and read it when we get back together in a group.

Debrief

How did you choose your team's main idea of your topic? How did your group brainstorm? Did people build on each other's ideas, or did they cut others off? How did the team come to consensus? How did you feel when you were done?

Variations

You can create a rap, a poem that rhymes every other line, a rhyming greeting card, spoken word, slam poetry, or a multitude of other poetry formats that the team can deliver together.

Case Study

Team Haiku takes editing to a level beyond mechanics; teams usually begin developing structures for creating, editing, and deleting together. This is useful in that it forces the team members to establish norms using the cursor placement and the chat window on the side. One team began writing on the topic of why we engage in team building. One person would type and then another cursor would jump in and type when there was a pause. Another person found the comment feature by right-clicking (on a Mac, hold down Control while clicking):

Other team members soon caught on to either support a word or section or to voice new opinions. Other members used the chat window to give general feedback or carry on side conversations.

This turned into a great exercise of consensus. Although it took longer to do it this way than if one person had written it, this approach was much more powerful—because multiple people with multiple points of view chose and reviewed each syllable. I didn't capture their actual poem, but the following is an example of a draft poem with multiple comments and iterations leading to a final version.

Team Case Study—Simultaneous Team Editing

Time: 1–2 hours

Participants: 2–50 (current simultaneous limit on Google) per team; unlimited teams.

Technology: Internet, Google Docs or another application that allows simultaneous editing

Category: Collaboration

Goals

Get new or existing teams to massively collaborate and learn how to use multiple online tools and channels of communication to write a case study entirely online without talking to your teammates.

Game Summary

Case studies are a great way to access and apply the collective knowledge of a large group while having team members complete a task that ends with a real work product. You can use this activity for large events with multiple teams as a way to display collaboration in action.

Setup

Prepare the case study and upload to a shared location such as Google Docs. Post the link to the materials up to seven days before the actual team-building event.

Instructions to the Audience

Today we are going to work collaboratively to create a single page of recommendations on how to cut a (fictitious) $1,000,000 annual budget by 50 percent. You will have 75 minutes to choose an appropriate collaborative online tool, divvy up the work, discuss options, make decisions, and write the report. (Take 10 minutes as well to review the case study's location and details.) Oh, and here's the final rule: You can't talk to each other face to face! You must conduct all communication online. We'll take 30 minutes at the end to discuss your results and the process face to face and over video conference.

Power Tips

Use http://coveritlive.com as a live blogging technique that can also capture all of the online communication to be used in the debriefing and for sharing the learning for future sessions. Have one person represent the client; allow participants to talk to and ask questions of this client as a way to clarify the assignment. The client can also add new information at key points to either move progress along or add additional challenges.

Be prepared to facilitate success and failure.

Facilitator Notes

Allow the group to find its own way. Interject only if you think they really need help working together or need a suggestion to get through a block. Asking questions is the preferred method for attempting to help the team.

Debrief

What were you thinking in the first 20 minutes? What tool did you choose? How did you resolve conflicts?

Did a leader emerge? What is something you noticed in the results that you'll use back at work?

Case Study

Conferences That Work author Adrian Segar blogged about how Joel Backon of Choate Rosemary Hall School used this unique initiative at edACCESS 2010, a conference for the association of information technology at small independent schools. Joel did the preliminary work in defining and uploading the case study materials and then set the stage for 40 people who were meeting live to work virtually for 90 minutes! Although many people weren't sure whether they could finish in the first 20 minutes, the group selected a spreadsheet to use in Google Docs, and the majority of people began working on this. It had multiple tabs and was clearly able to document 60 percent savings. With just 30 minutes to go, the group of 40 created a Google Doc of the case study summary to augment the spreadsheet. With a completed Case Study document and supporting spreadsheet, the group was able to complete the assignment in just 90 minutes. This was an incredible example of teamwork specific to these 40 participants working under a tight deadline. It also shows the power that online collaboration can have if harnessed correctly.

See other articles on how college students are using this feature to tag team class note-taking and think about what team applications it could be used for in meetings and team trainings.

Link to @asegar[3] article about using this team building game in the 2010 conference: http://www.conferencesthatwork.com/index.php/event-design/2010/06/innovative-participatory-conference-session-a-case-study-using-online-tools/

Link to Huffington Post article on using Google Docs to collaborate on taking notes: http://www.huffingtonpost.com/hack-college/use-google-docs-to-collab_b_844192.html

Link to article about using online collaboration for Cross-Team work: http://curbservice.wordpress.com/2011/08/23/using-online-collaboration-for-cross-team-work-google-docs-zotero/

---

[3]Many thanks to @asegar for publishing this article, which includes links to the case study, log, and debrief.

CHAPTER

8

EPIC Team Building

Today I went on thesaurus.com *and searched "ninjas." The computer told me "Ninjas cannot be found." Well played, ninjas, well played.*

—epicquotes.com

EPIC Digital Team Building Challenges push the envelope of just team building and approach the realm of full-blown productions. They also take a significant amount of time to plan. Some of these initiatives can take from days to months to plan, depending on their scale. The return on this effort is a transformational experience that can serve as the catalyst for changing a team's actions or culture. They leave a lasting impression—a lifelong memory that enables participants to recognize that a team took the extra effort, from the small details to the overall event to create an amazing learning experience.

There are, of course, countless creative initiatives beyond what is discussed in this book—and you can "EPIC'ize" many of the digital team-building experiences in this book by taking them a step further. For instance, the research division of a software company lent us a new video camera in one of our events; this camera was able to overlay arrows, markers, and messages into a physical environment and then add them to the video itself. So when you view the video, it includes what looks like floating messages inside the video screen. We used this to lead a team from a door through four hallways. We placed a critical piece of information floating in the video camera of augmented reality in a large 10-story atrium. It was EPIC, to say the least.

The pace of technology and access to that technology continues to grow, so keep an eye on trends (and our blog!) to spot the latest in successful digital team-building events.

141

SCVNGR—GPS Treasure Hunt for Team Building and Cross-Team Collaboration

Time: 1–4+ hours

Participants: 2–12 per team; nearly infinite number of teams

Technology: Web and GPS-enabled cell phone

Category: EPIC team building, collaboration, strategy, problem solving, flexibility

Goals

Create an EPIC team-building event and increase team communication, trust, and planning by creating a customized game on a highly used, location-based gaming platform.

Game Summary

After receiving four rounds of venture funding, SCVNGR is becoming one of the biggest location-based gaming platforms around. The idea behind this activity is that participants need to go somewhere and complete a challenge. In addition, they receive points for checking in, bumping phones with someone, writing a note, or taking a photo.

Setup

1. Go to scvngr.com and click Log In on top right:

2. Register for a new account:

3. Enter info and click Register.

4. Click Builder at the top:

5. Click Treks:

Welcome, John!

Challenges   Rewards   Treks

6. Click Create Trek:

Welcome, John!

Challenges   Rewards   **Treks**

Displaying 1 trek   Create Trek

7. Enter your event information and click Save and Continue:

8. Click Add Another Challenge:

9. Click Select Place:

10. You can attempt to search for an existing location or click Add a new place if it's not listed on your first search.

Not finding what you want? **Add a new place.**

11. You can search by address, or if you have a GPS waypoint, you can plug that into the street address field and click Center Map to confirm you have the right location. Once you have the right location, click Submit.

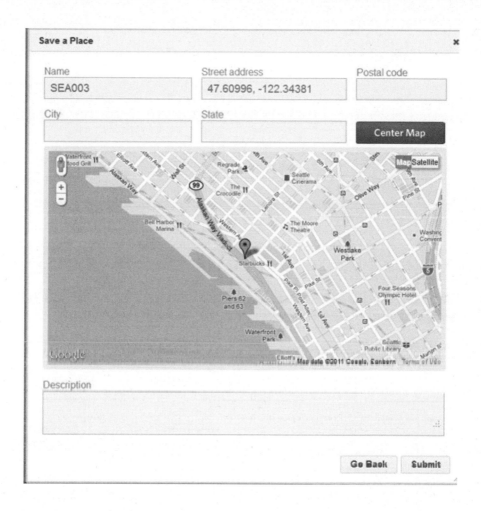

12. Complete the information for this activity. You can assign 2 to 5 points per challenge, require a correct answer, have an open answer, create a photo challenge, or have team members scan a QR code to prove they were there. Click Save when you're done.

≡ New Challenge

Basic Info

Place ⓘ   SEA003   **Select Place**

Title ⓘ   May Or or May Not

Points ⓘ   2   ▤ ────────────────────────

Challenge ⓘ   Who was the mayor of Seattle in 1984?

Challenge ⓘ   Specific Text Response   ▼
Type
                   Enter all acceptable answers separated by commas, we'll handle misspellings.

Answers ⓘ   charles royer

- Multimedia

Image   Cancel C:\Users\John Chen\Documents\2 **Browse...**

Audio/Video   No attachment | Edit

- Messages

Done Message   Take a government inspired photo.

Incorrect Message Try Again! Use all lower case, 2 words.

Fail Message

13. Make sure to click "activate" next to your challenge to turn it on.

14. Repeat for all of your challenges.
15. E-mail all of your participants and make sure at least one person per team downloads the SCVNGR app and can log in correctly.

The goal here is to educate your teams about facts, have them complete small team challenges, gather photos of team behavior, and gain additional value in other ways during this hunt—all while providing a fun and engaging experience for employees. To help ensure a fair start, you can deactivate your hunt until the event's actual start time.

Instructions to the Audience

You are going on a high-tech scavenger hunt, and your goal is to score more points than any other team. The top team will win a prize. Start your SCVNGR app on your cell phone and look at Treks for the trek we have created for you. This trek has information on all of your challenges. By clicking Activity, you can see when the last team scored, and clicking Info will display the team rankings. You must stay together as a team; we will determine whether you have successfully completed all of the challenges. You have a fixed amount of time to complete this hunt and will be disqualified if you are late.

Debrief

Did the teams ask any clarifying questions about the goals or the rules? Did they spend any time planning before they left? How did the team work together? Did they naturally fall into roles, or did they split up into small factions and have disharmony? How well did they recover if something challenging happened? How did they alter their strategy if they knew they were behind? Did they just keep doing the same thing? Or did they simply give up? How much did they talk to other teams? Did they use cell phones? Did they talk to each other if they bumped into each other? How did some of the specific challenge relate to what they do at work? Mark any teams that arrive late. What does this represent in terms of their work?

Case Study

SCVNGR is being used for University Campus Tours. Instead of the usual walk and talk campus tour, many schools are putting together a competitive interactive game that allows potential students to become familiar with the campus *and* gives their school a high-tech brand edge. The students engage in team building and get to know some of their potential classmates during the tour. In addition, the prize for the winning team is priority processing for all of their students! This is a valuable advantage in this competitive academic market where many more students are applying for fewer open positions.

This is a video of a university using SCVNGR for a University Campus Tour; click the third video to the right for the University of Louisville: http://www.scvngr.com/university/.

Geoteaming—GPS Treasure Hunt for Team Building and Cross-Team Collaboration

Time: 2–4+ hours

Participants: 2–12 per team; nearly infinite number of teams

Technology: GPS, Web-enabled cell phone, digital camera

Category: EPIC team building, collaboration, strategy, problem solving, flexibility

Goals

Teams learn valuable team-building and cross-team collaboration skills by scoring the most points by finding geocaches (questions or containers hidden in a specific location) and balancing the goals: that all teams find all the locations at least once and maximize points.

Game Summary

First executed by Dr. Simon Priest in England as a framework for navigating between team-building in the 1990s, Geoteaming began using this idea in 2001, a year after the GPS signal was descrambled for civilian use. This created a recreational sport called Geocaching (http://geocaching.com). As of February 2012, there were more than 1,642,011 active geocaches in the world, with millions of players—and this number is growing daily. Geoteaming and Geocaching formed a partnership to develop events based on Geocaching, and they held the first related team-building event in Seattle, Washington—in Discovery Park (630 acres in the city!). They worked together with computer software company Adobe and completed six events in 2001. Since then, more than 950 events with 50,000 participants—averaging 100 to 140 events per year—have been produced, and that signifies a hit in the training world. Although the framework is simple and allows customizations, Geoteaming can lead to very complex dynamics and amazing experiences. Some events went deep into bringing their corporate values to life, and some pushed the boundary of adventure with caches that resulted in learning how to do a backflip off a 30-foot trapeze and going on a helicopter ride *under* the Golden Gate Bridge!

Setup

Get a digital camera and a GPS receiver. (We'll assume you have a Garmin eTrex H, which costs about $80. It is the easiest and least expensive GPS to buy. There are also apps such as MotionX GPS for $2.99 and others that can turn your smartphone into a GPS.) Begin at your starting point; walk around and choose locations to either hide a physical container (use clear Tupperware or other containers that will *not* be mistaken for anything suspicious should others accidentally find it!) with a code word in it; alternatively, use an area that has an answer to a question (such as a historical plaque). We usually create 20 locations; although you can use fewer for a smaller event, a good guideline is to have at least one location per team.

Mark the waypoint by selecting Menu > Mark. This should automatically give it the name "001," but you can change the name as you like and then select OK. Take a photograph of an item nearby that you can use as a clue; write the question (or hint) that will help a team find this location when they get close. Then place the container if you are putting one here. Since GPS is accurate to approximately 30 feet, a photographic and written clue are both needed to help teams figure out what they're looking for.

When you have all of your locations, download all of your photos and use our Word document template to create a clue sheet, inserting your pictures and clues and assigning a point value for each location. Assign fewer points to locations that are close and easy; award more point for those that are far away or challenging (such as those that contain a puzzle, have two or more stages, etc.). Finally, program all the GPS receivers (at least one per team) with the coordinates you have. If you don't want to manually enter all this information, we suggest you purchase a download cable and use a program such as EasyGPS to download the information from your GPS and upload it to all of your other GPS receivers. Higher-end GPS receivers use a mini-USB cable to conduct downloads and uploads. You can see how all of these steps and physical work truly make this an EPIC team-building event.

Instructions to the Audience

You are going on a high-tech treasure hunt. Your goal is to score more points than any other team, with the top team winning a prize. In addition, if all the teams get to *all* the locations at least once, you win a company prize—something for everybody.

There are five key rules:

1. Your team must stay together; you can't split up and go in two different directions.
2. No running is allowed.
3. You must take a photo of all of your teammates except your photographer at each cache.
4. Follow all traffic and pedestrian laws.
5. You must arrive before the return time. If you are more than 1 second late according to the GPS, your team will lose *half* of its points!

We'll show you how to GOTO a waypoint. There are five buttons to learn on this GPS receiver.

1. Press and hold the bottom right circular Power button until you see someone walk across your screen.

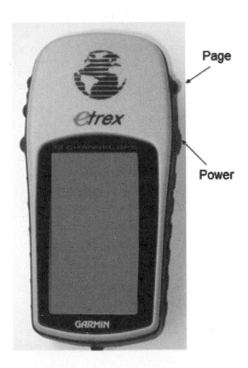

2. Press multiple times the top right Page button and see it cycle through a set of screens. If you're trying to go to the next waypoint, press the Page button until the word MENU appears at the top.

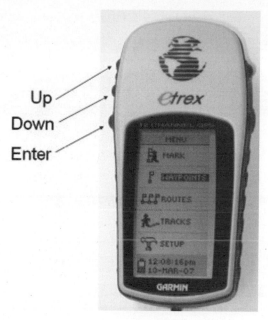

Up

Down

Enter

3. The next two buttons are the up and down buttons on the top left. Press the down button until the word Waypoints is highlighted.

4. Press the Enter button, and you'll see a set of index tabs on your left. Press the down arrow until you see your waypoints. (We have them all start with three letters, such as GEO for Geoteaming.)

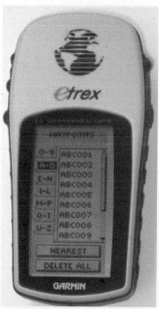

5. Press the Enter button again and the cursor will go from the left to the right.

6. Let's pretend your team chose to go to GEO008. Press the down arrow until GEO008 is highlighted.

7. Press the Enter button; it will say REVIEW WAYPOINT, and GOTO will be highlighted.

8. Press Enter again; if you're connected to satellites, you'll see you waypoint number at the top. This indicates the distance away in miles or feet and an arrow in the direction that the cache is hidden. Remember, these GPS receivers need movement, so hold it in front of you and start walking in a straight line; it will then "lock" on and give you a correct reading.

Any questions?

If not, let's meet outside to connect the GPS receivers; then we'll start the game clock. (We suggest using the clocks on the GPS receivers as the game clock because they are all synchronized.)

Debrief

Did the teams ask any clarifying questions about the goals or the rules? Did the teams get completely competitive, or did they attempt to work with other teams toward a company goal? How did the teams work together? Did they naturally fall into roles, or did they split up in groups and have disharmony? How well did they recover when something happened? How did teams alter their strategies if they knew they were behind? Did they just give up? How much did they talk to other teams? Did they use cell phones? Did they talk to each other if they bumped into each other? What did they learn about cross-team collaboration? Make sure the teams arrive back on time and mark any teams that come in late; then divide their score in half. What does coming back late represent in their work?

Case Study[1]

A very interesting fact is that only seven teams (less than 1 percent) of the 950 companies that have played this event have achieved the highest score possible. During one event for a group of federal agency leaders, one participant essentially gave a speech about the "correct" answer to collaboration for the activity in front of the entire crowd. Her speech was amazing, and my team and I waited anxiously in the back of the room to see what would happen. The other two teams looked at each other briefly and then proceeded to say, "Nah, we're going to do our own thing." It was *mind blowing* to watch a team throw away the right answer. During the debrief 3 hours later, I was able to alert everyone to the fact that she did indeed have the right answer after I announced the winner. Although this woman could certainly stand to improve her persuasion skills, the other two teams *definitely* got the message that they needed to pay attention to out-of-the-box solutions and support collaborations that benefit everybody involved.

During another event, for REI (one of the world's largest retailers), the team arrived at the highest solution possible after a full day of Geoteaming. This led five departments who worked under one roof to start experimenting wildly with cross-product collaboration. The approach they ending up using was similar to Amazon's concept called "what other people bought," a strategy in which you group or place items that sell together. The result was that two or more departments started collaborating by placing items that sell together. For instance, if you were buying a GPS, perhaps you'd also buy a walking stick and a book on

---

[1]*Source:* Priest, S. & Rohnke, K. #101 of *101 of the Best Corporate Team-Building Activities*, 2nd ed. (Tacoma, WA: Tarrak Technologies, 2000). http://www.tarrak.com/BOOKS/101.htm

Geocaching. The collaboration led to higher add-on sales as products from two or more areas were sold together, equating to more money spent. As a result, this company went on to enjoy one of their highest revenue years in history, despite the challenging economy.

Flash Mobs—Organize Your Team in Time and Space

Time: 5–20 minutes; hours of organization

Participants: minimum of 10

Technology: Internet, social media, video

Category: EPIC team building, collaboration, creativity, communication, training

Goals

Create an EPIC team-building event featuring collaboration, timing, communication, and shared performance goals as 10 or more people work together to assemble suddenly in a public place, perform an unusual act, and then disperse.

Game Summary

The term *flash mob* was coined in 2003 and has since reached pop culture status in advertising. It makes for a great video and experience at an event; the secret is that it requires a lot of planning and team building to happen correctly. Although many flash mobs feature dancing and singing, others have included freezing (not moving for a period of time) and even off-the-wall events like pillow fights. What's key to the power of a flash mob is the collaboration and synchronicity of many people doing the same thing—something we all know is very challenging to achieve in everyday life.

Setup

An organizing team must create the experience you're trying to make, such as having a team of 300 do a synchronized dance in the cafeteria on a particular day and at a specific time. Then the team needs to work on training for the dance. You can hold the training live. Or you can train people online by using a video to teach people the dance. You then have to start recruiting by putting out marketing/messages and having people sign up and complete the training. Many organizations also use either e-mail or group texting to inform the group of any upcoming changes to times or dates. Organized flash mobs will usually have at least one live rehearsal in an offsite location if possible before the main performance.

Instructions to the Audience

We are going to create a flash mob, which is a group of people who assemble suddenly in a public place, perform an unusual act for a brief time, and then disperse. Let's start taking ideas on what the goal of the flash mob is and what it should be and then start planning who is going to do what.

Debrief

Who takes leadership? How does the group create order and planning in a new task? Who is engaged and who is not? How does the group create support and get others to buy into the idea? What helps the most in execution? What did the team learn from working together? What was the result of the flash mob?

Case Study

Although most flash mobs are for entertainment, you can also use these as a powerful vehicle for changing behavior. What's great about them as well is that the resulting video can go viral after it's created and continue to have an impact long after the event has ended. Another interesting fact is that many people get emotional watching flash mobs—due to their beauty, their message, their power, or whatever other reason that makes us human. For example, one unknown group had the goal of improving recycling in Quebec. The video they created (link follows) moved me to tears, as it had an unexpected ending for which I was completely unprepared. It also conveys some great facts and will hopefully increase the number of people in the world who recycle. Now that's global teamwork.

http://www.washingtonpost.com/blogs/blogpost/post/flash-mob-teaches-recycling-lessons-video/2011/06/07/AGn1kFLI I_blog.html

Another good idea is Improv Everywhere's Mp3 experiments. By using this idea, you can create an Mp3 that includes training information and then get everyone to download it and play it at the exact same time. Improv Everywhere was able to get 3,000 people to come together for Experiment 7: http://www.youtube.com/watch?v=kVuVhcdQs0k.

CHAPTER 9

Closers—Ending a Team-Building Event

I am a member of a team, and I rely on the team, I defer to it and sacrifice for it, because the team, not the individual, is the ultimate champion.

—Mia Hamm, Gold Medal Soccer Champion

Closers are important in team-building events because they cite the conclusion of the official time during which teams hone their skills. Hopefully, they also highlight the importance of ending on a positive note and provide valuable takeaways for each team member.

It's important that closers be inclusive (giving every person the opportunity to contribute) and make it clear that the group process is coming to an end so that people can leave afterward. It's also essential that this part of the process make the team feel as though the experience was positive, was an effective use of their time, and gave them the chance to develop skills that would help them improve at work.

Technology allows increasingly larger-sized audiences to be included in team-building events these days, especially in an appropriate or shorter amount of time. Be sure to end with one of these closers and be one of the 20 percent who actually follow up after a team-building event to maximize the investment you've made.

Shout-Outs—Acknowledging Teammates

Time: 10–20 minutes

Participants: 2–1,000

Technology: Twitter, text, chat, teleconference (optional)

Category: Closers

Goals

Create team bonding and event closure by having one teammate acknowledge another teammate for his or her contributions to the team-building session.

Game Summary

As one of my good friends, Helice Bridges (blueribbons.com), says, not only are people hungry for food; they are hungry for acknowledgment. The following simple closing activity gives each person the chance to take the time to acknowledge his or her teammates for their contributions. This raises team morale, enhances relations among people, and allows the receivers to notice something about themselves they may not normally see.

Setup

Continue using an event hashtag or use your existing text or chat connection for this closing initiative. You can arrange an optional teleconference or conduct the event live to increase the speed of giving directions and of the debriefing session.

Instructions to the Audience

Acknowledgment from your teammates is a crucial way to increase team morale and connections. In addition, feedback can let you know what actions you're taking that benefit the team. Select one to three teammates to whom you'd like to send a message, either by using their username or real name. Cite something specific that they did during this team-building session that you recognized. For example, "Holly, thank you for knowing the by-laws in depth to keep our team out of legal troubles."

Debrief

Take the time to read through the results and highlight a few of the posts. In addition, you can ask the receiving person what he or she thought or felt in receiving the acknowledgments.

Case Study

We did this closing during a team-building event where one woman posted that she was so grateful to the team—one person in particular who had helped her through her recent medical challenges. She mentioned how emotional she was from that support, and the team responded with even more support for her. This showed the critical piece of team building: supporting her in her personal life as well as her professional life. It also built a strong team culture, in that members were not reluctant to show how much they cared for one another. Every team member felt proud of the fact that they were able to help this woman. They responded by acknowledging how much she had given to the team and the company and assuring her that they were glad to help her when she needed it.

"I Commit to . . . "—Public Commitment to Change

Time: 10–20 minutes
Participants: 2–1,000
Technology: Twitter, text, chat, teleconference (optional)
Category: Closers

Goals

Create an individual action plan and commitment to create a tangible close to a team-building event. This can increase team commitment and personal responsibility, creating an improved work environment.

Game Summary

I received this initiative from Dr. Simon Priest, and find it to be one of the easiest ways to effectively follow up at the end of a program. Revisiting these commitments within two to four weeks after the team-building session has the potential to help members retain 80 percent of the team-building gains. In addition, by committing publicly to your team, you increase the odds that the individual will own the action.

Setup

Continue using an event hashtag or use your existing text or chat connection for this closing initiative. You can arrange an optional teleconference or complete this activity live to make the direction-giving and debriefing periods move more quickly.

Instructions to the Audience

One of the goals of this training is not simply to learn a lot; it's also to take something from this training and use it to *do* something differently. Knowledge itself is not power; new actions and results are power. And the choices you make each day are in your complete control. So to gain the value of this training, decide on one thing you'll commit to do to be either a better team player or team leader. Start your post with "I commit to..."

Power Tips

You can use free online tools such as HootSuite Archives to archive all of your results to remind people of their commitments (or you can simply cut and paste into a document). One great tip is to send these e-mails two to four weeks after the event. You can do it just prior to the next team meeting to remind everyone of their commitments and then follow up on the results of those commitments during that next meeting.

Debrief

Take the time to read through the results and highlight a few of the posts. In listening to the debriefs, as the facilitator, you can begin to influence or model the level of commitments that everyone will bring to this event. Look for SMART (specific, measurable, attainable, realistic, timely) goals and ask questions such as:

How specifically will you do that?

How could you measure that commitment?

What would have to happen for you to feel like you upheld your commitment?

What is a tangible goal along the way that you can realistically obtain by our next meeting?

When will you complete your commitment by?

Which commitment got the most audience reaction?

Which commitment did you think was the most sincere?

Which commitment was most specific in creating a tangible work result?

Case Study[1]

During one team-building event, a teammate who was in charge of increasing cash flow made a commitment to work with three different teams to decrease the time of a process that

---

[1]*Sources:* Priest, S. #95 and #100 of *100 of the Best Virtual Team-Building Events*. (Seattle, WA: Tarrak Technologies, 2001). virtualteamworks.com; http://www.tarrak.com/BOOKS/100.htm

Priest, S., Sikes, S. & Evans, F. #83 of *99 of the Best Experiential Corporate Games We Know*. (Lakebay, WA: eXperientia, 2000). http://www.tarrak.com/BOOKS/99.htm

typically took 4 hours. This employee had to personally visit each salesperson to receive a status update on every project in terms of accounting. Because the company was already using a Customer Relationship Management (CRM) system such as salesforce.com, this individual met with leaders from sales, accounting, and operations and mapped out the workflow process for five different accounting stages per project. In addition, he measured how long it stayed in each stage so that he could track and hold each team accountable. Finally, he rolled out this workflow with buy-in from each of the teams. Amazingly, cash flow from closed projects improved from 64 days to 32 days on average, and the process to get the information went from 4 hours to *1 second* with the push of a button!

A summary of research on follow-up and self-facilitation training after a team-building event can be found at: http://geoteaming.com/georesearch.pdf.

Just Three Words—Micro-Assessing Your Team

Time: 5–20 minutes

Participants: 2–1,000

Technology: Twitter, text, chat, teleconference (optional)

Category: Closer

Goals

Gain team status and feedback at the end of a team-building event to determine how the team views the event in just three words. Close the team-building event with positive words.

Game Summary

Teammates reflect on the team-building or meeting experience and sum up their thoughts in just three words.

Setup

Continue using an event hashtag or use your existing text or chat connection for this closing initiative. You can arrange a teleconference or conduct the event live to speed up the direction-giving and debriefing processes.

Instructions to the Audience

It's time to close this training, and we want to find out where everyone is before we close this team-building game. Take a moment to think about all that you learned and sum up your experience in just three words. Send your three words via text, chat, or Twitter, and I'll read some of them after a few minutes.

Debrief

Take the time to read through the results and highlight a few of the posts, especially ones with thought-provoking words. Close by thanking all your participants, and then end your training session.

Case Study

One team took the three-word close to the extreme. They were still experiencing the high morale that resulted from solving a very complex team-building challenge. Three-word quotes came streaming in: "Never give up," "Success is yours," "Anything is possible," "I heart team," and "Dreams come true," along with other powerful messages. The trainer was moved that he was able to help this team so much, and he closed this event. A week later, a package arrived in the mail for this trainer. He opened the package and found this necklace that a team member had created on http://zazzle.com:

(You can use other sites like CafePress.com that can turn anything into a physical object.) He also saw the note that the participant had sent with the necklace: "THANK YOU for your gifts and skills as a trainer. Our team was on a path to failure and with your help, I can tell you that the last week was one of my BEST weeks working with this team. We knew we had the potential; thank you for seeing it, believing in it and most of all, making it come true. Dreams DO come true."

Digital Slideshow—Picture Your Success

Time: 5–10 minutes

Participants: 2–1,000

Technology: Screen sharing via Web conferencing, teleconference (optional)

Category: Closers

Goals

This activity provides a way to see how much progress a team made during a training session and allows the team to reflect on the results and the people who made it happen.

Game Summary

Digital slideshows continue to be an easy and effective tool for reflection. There is something primal in the way that people like to see themselves in photos, and this is a great way to compress the entire training into just a few minutes. You can also turn the slideshow into a video or other production to allow the training to continue into the future.

Setup

Start a Web conference using BuddyMeeting.com or another screen-sharing service. Obtain photos throughout the event by having participants send you pictures of themselves (this could be done as an icebreaker) and of their teams if they are participating in remote locations. You can also take screen shots of the team-building initiatives you completed at different stages by using PrtSc (PrintScreen; usually located on the top right of a Windows keyboard) and saving it in a drawing program such as Paint (pbrush.exe, Edit > Paste after pressing PrtSc). (On a Mac, press Shift+Command+4 to take a screen shot.) Save all the photos into one directory and be sure that you know how to view them all as a slideshow. It may be helpful to have a technical assistant to help with this on another computer so that you can focus on facilitation; then the assistant can provide all the pictures on a flash drive. In addition, you can play music from a player, Pandora.com, or another music source while exhibiting the pictures. Rehearse with a set of test photos to make sure you can do it live.

Instructions to the Audience

Let's take a moment to review all that we've done. We've collected photos that you've sent us and took some during today's training. We're going to show these photos in a slideshow as a way to recap the day. If you like a particular photo, then please write your comments in the chat window. We'll help judge the best photo of the day.

Debrief

Write notes during the slideshow about what you consider to be the best photos of the day and make a note of which ones got the most reactions from your team. After the slideshow, return to the teleconference and compliment some of the most popular photos. Then announce the "best photo of the day" and potentially give extra accolades or a gift to the winning team.

Case Study

In a recent GooseChase cell phone scavenger hunt, more than 1,700 high school students involved in a program called DECA produced over 3,900 photos in 2½ hours. One team displayed a gem of a moment as they staged this scene of two gentlemen shaving and washing their hair in a plaza fountain while six women made the DECA logo with their fingers. One teammate posted it on Facebook and got 100 "Likes" in less than 60 minutes. If our youth has the guts and creativity to pull this photo off and can channel this kind of energy to make this world a better place, I know we're in good hands.

APPENDIX: GETTING ONLINE

This following is a step-by-step guide for accessing our commonly used resources. Please note that the pace of change in technology is extraordinarily fast and these instructions can change. See http://50digitalteambuildinggames.com for updates on instructions.

Twitter

1. Go to http://twitter.com.
2. Click Sign up:

3. a. Make sure your information checks out.
   b. Passwords with numbers, letters, and special characters, such as IL0veTw1tter, are the strongest passwords.

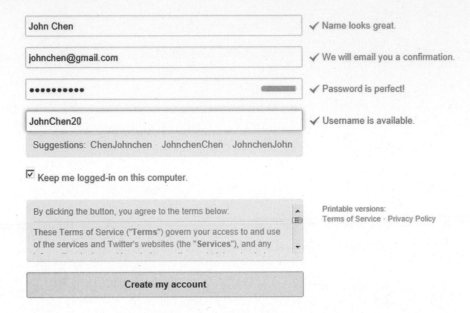

4. Select interests to start getting tweets from people you are interested in.

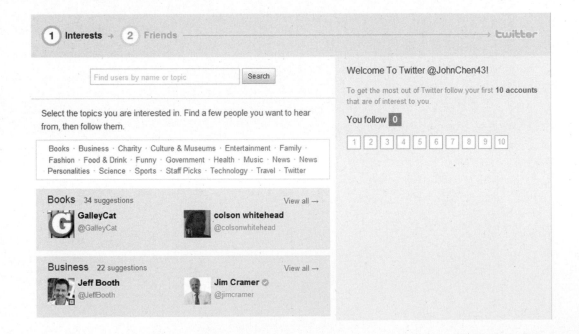

5. Import your friends.

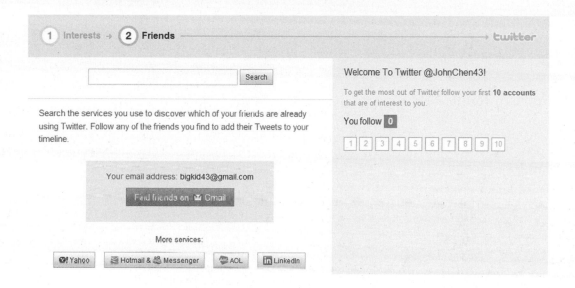

6. Click in the What's happening? box and then write your first tweet!

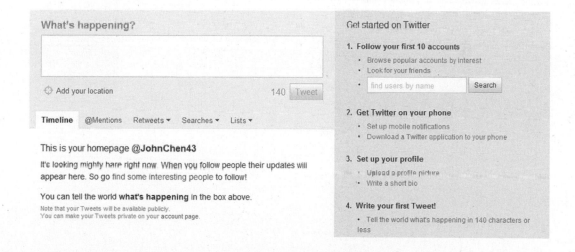

7. Click in the search box and type in a hashtag or a phrase that you are looking for (e.g., #techieteams or teambuilding) and click the magnifying glass to search for all tweets with that word in it.

FreeConference.com

This site has won numerous awards, including PC World's Best Free Stuff All Time Greats. I have conducted more than 100 teleconferences with this service with almost no problems. I use Conferences On Demand so I just use one phone number and reuse the PIN as many times as possible; it's programmed into my phone, and after a while, I had committed it to memory.

1. Go to freeconference.com.
2. Click Sign Up:

3. Fill in the information on the Sign Up screen.

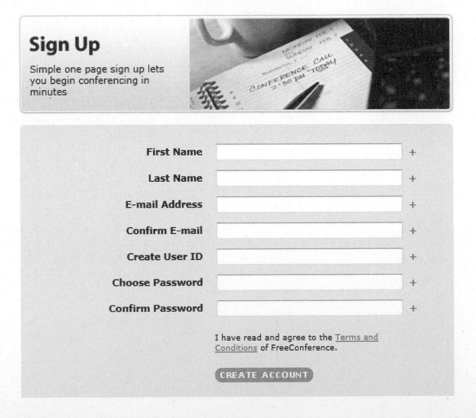

4. Go to your e-mail program and look for your activation link.

Thank you for Signing Up!

Your new account has been created, and an activation link
has been sent from accounts@freeconference.com to the
email address you provided: geoteaming@gmail.com

Don't see the email?
Please check your spam folder, resend email or
sign up using a different email address.

5. Click on the activation link.

For security purposes, you must validate your email in order to activate your
account.

Click Here to Activate Your FreeConference.com Account

If you cannot click on the hyperlink, please copy and paste the following URL
into your browser:
https://www.freeconference.com/Activate.ashx?p=
8910C766AA0ED5DE475DD96BA2220E05

Please note, you will not be able to use FreeConference.com until you have
activated your account.

Best Regards,

Your FreeConference.com Team

6. And get your Conference On Demand number you can use for all your teleconferences.

Conference On Demand

DEDICATED DIAL-IN NUMBER
1 (540) 712-0350

ACCESS CODE
339-6524

Provide participants with
dial-in number, access code,
and date and time of your
call. Use anywhere, anytime
for on-the-go conferencing.

Facebook

With ultimate back-channel capability, multiperson chat, video, and 50 million-plus people, Facebook can be used for many of the initiatives in this book.

1. Go to Facebook.com and fill in the Sign Up form.

Sign Up

It's free and always will be.

First Name: [   ]

Last Name: [   ]

Your Email: [   ]

Re-enter Email: [   ]

New Password: [   ]

I am: [Select Sex: ▼]

Birthday: [Month: ▼] [Day: ▼] [Year: ▼]

Why do I need to provide my birthday?

Sign Up

2. After verifying your account by e-mail, add your teammates.
3. You can communicate with your team by posting status updates, photos, or videos or by asking a question (a version of a poll).

📄 **Update Status**   📷 **Add Photo / Video**   ▤ **Ask Question**

4. You can create multiperson chats or video calls by clicking on the person's name on the bottom right. To add people, click the gear icon and select Add Friends to Chat.... You can click the video camera to start a video chat with that person.

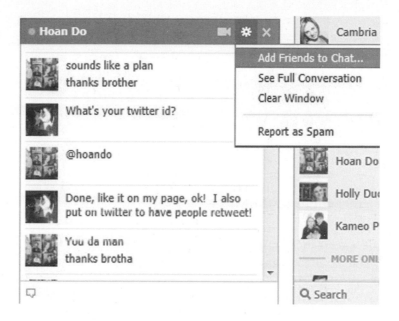

5. There is a lot of functionality with Facebook and many Facebook apps that you can use to stay connected with your team.

Google Docs

Google Docs is a great *free* collaborative tool that has capability for up to 50 people to work together in real time. You can use it as a platform for digital team-building games to create an almost unlimited number of activities. You can also use it to search the Web for people who have created and shared other games.

1. Go to gmail.com and click Create An Account.

2. Fill in your information to create an account and click on I accept, create my account.

3. Click the Show me my Account button.

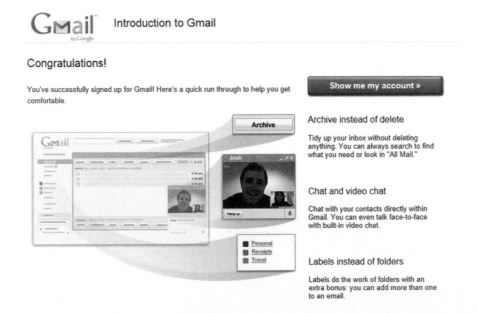

4. Click Documents in the top toolbar.

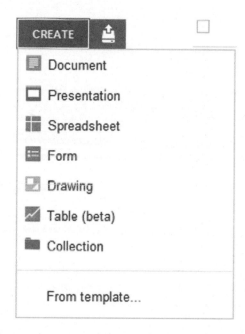

5. Click Create to create your first document.

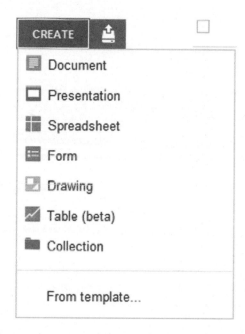

6. You can follow the instructions for creating and sharing documents in the team-building games.

Google+ and Google Hangouts

In response to Facebook's popularity, Google introduced Google+ and included Google Hangouts, which is currently one of the best multiperson video conferencing tools available. It can hold up to 10 simultaneous video chats and allows users to share screens, videos, and documents, among its other capabilities. Google+ also has status updates, chat capability, and many other features that you can use in conjunction with the digital team-building games in this book.

1. Once logged in to Gmail, click +You in the top right corner.

2. Click Join.

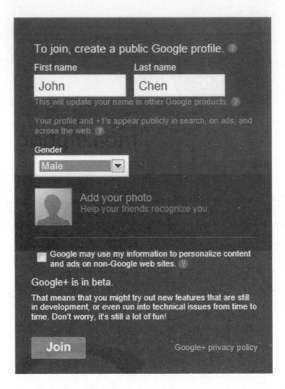

3. Add friends connecting to an online e-mail account. The Circles feature allows you to add friends to different levels. I would recommend starting with one circle, but you can define a personal and professional circle and expand from there.

4. Click Start a hangout.

5. Invite people to your hangout.

6. Use the available features, such as chat, video conferencing, or YouTube sharing of videos.

BuddyMeeting

BuddyMeeting is one of the best *free* Web conferencing services that I've found on the Internet. Although there are many other sites, this one is fast, downloads quickly, has great performance, and is free. It has real-time chat capability, can upload any PowerPoint document (there can be some conversion challenges with some documents), can do live whiteboarding, can share your screen or Web cam, and has the ability to pass control to participants or allow them to raise their hands. That's a lot of features for free Web conferencing.

1. Go to http://buddymeeting.com and click Sign-Up!

Welcome **Guest, Sign-Up!**

2. You can log in by creating a new account or using Google or Facebook to log in.

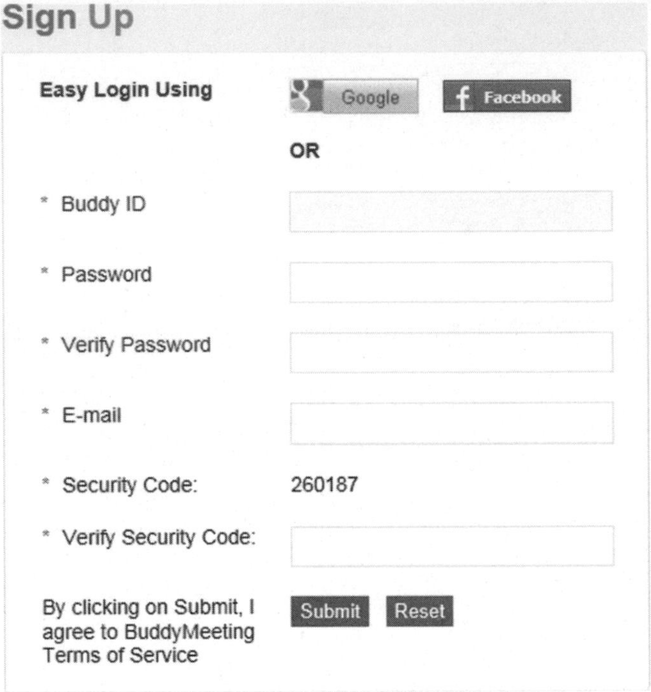

Sign Up

Easy Login Using   [Google]   [f Facebook]

OR

* Buddy ID

* Password

* Verify Password

* E-mail

* Security Code: 260187

* Verify Security Code:

By clicking on Submit, I   [Submit] [Reset]
agree to BuddyMeeting
Terms of Service

3. Click Create Meeting.

Welcome bigkid, Click your option below

- Create Meeting

- My Meetings

- Join Meeting

- My Profile

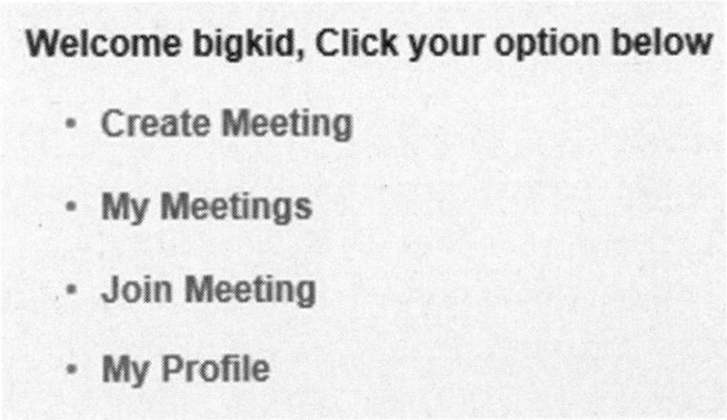

4. Be sure to verify your password and enter the meeting phone number if you're using a teleconference; then click Create.

Create New Meeting!

| * Meeting Description | New Meeting Topic | * Meeting Phone | 800-123-4567 | Need Phone# ? |

* Meeting Password   123456   * Phone Passcode   1234

* Verify Password   123456| * Meeting Agenda   Following items to be discussed :

* Start Date   11/14/2011

* Start Time   08:00:00 ▼ Hours

* Duration   01 Hr 00 Min   ➡ Create

convenience. Please change appropriately.   **Note:** The above values are pre-filled with defaults, for your

5. You'll receive an e-mail, or you can cut and paste this information and send it to your attendees to log in a few minutes before your meeting starts. *Be sure* to test this in your environment to ensure that firewalls or other technologies don't block your ability to meet.

Meeting successfully created !!

Meeting Details:
Meeting ID: 768269
Meeting Password: 123456
Meeting Description: New Meeting Topic
Meeting Start: 2011-11-14 08:00:00
Duration : 01 Hour(s) and 00 Minutes
Phone : 800-123-4567
Phone Passcode : 1234
Agenda : Following items to be discussed :

Click to Join

Email message successfully sent!!

Meeting details are also stored in **My Meetings** for your later use.

Participant Map

Participant Map - Team-Building Games with Technology
http://50digitalteambuildinggames.eventbrite.com

Name	Information	Time										

ABOUT GEOTEAMING

John Chen is the chief executive officer (CEO) of Geoteaming, a corporate team-building and leadership training firm that specializes in using technology and experiences to improve team and leadership performance. Combining 14 years of corporate team-building experience with 10 years of Microsoft experience, John creates innovative corporate team-building and leadership programs that create human change. During his 10 years at Microsoft, he helped ship 10 products, including leading eight teams to collaborate to ship Microsoft Exchange, which sold 100 million client licenses and earned 2 US patents. Geoteaming is a GPS-powered team-building event that uses a unique competitive-collaborative design to show collections of teams how to collaborate at a higher level. John continues to innovate with customized training and facilitations with the latest emerging technologies. John has been recognized as a Puget Sound Business Journal Top 40 Entrepreneur Under the Age of 40 and has received the BBB Innovative Business Practices Award and the 2008 *Training* magazine Top Young Trainer Award. He was the 2010 MPI Accredited Trainer and won the 2010 MPI Supplier of the Year. His clients include Booz Allen Hamilton, Microsoft, Adobe, Boeing, Motorola, and REI. You can reach John via e-mail at john@geoteaming.com, via phone, 877-652-0875; on Facebook, http://facebook.com/ceojohnchen; or on Twitter, @bigkid.

Team Building

Geoteaming offers a number of services to help clients build their teams.

Ah-Ha Geoteaming

This flagship 4-hour GPS program focuses on team building *and* cross-team collaboration. Using the high-tech treasure hunt sport of Geocaching, we'll build a custom course for you, and then your teams will attempt to find up to 700 or more will attempt to find as much as possible as the lessons for your team scoring the most and the company getting to all the locations are learned. With more than 50,000 satisfied customers, and events as large as 700 people.

GooseChase

Unlock teamwork, strategy, and creativity in this cell phone photo scavenger hunt that can be done *anywhere!*

GooseChase is a high-tech team-building event that uses your iOS, Droid, or BlackBerry phone to unlock teamwork, strategy, and hidden creativity.

Participants will download an app and log in to your customized photo scavenger hunt. Then you're off as you finish missions, collect photographic evidence, and upload. You'll receive Facebook-like status updates from all the teams and see your place in a real-time high score list, fueling your competitive spirit.

You'll return to debrief your core learning lessons, find out who won the prizes, and finally end with a digital slideshow of the best photos from the day.

Digital Team Building

We can lead any of the initiatives in this book and design custom initiatives using our expert facilitators to gain the value of team building. With the ability to create team building all around the world, with potentially no travel and expenses, this option can be highly effective with your organizations.

We offer a series of webinars throughout the year; check our website for upcoming programs.

Team Consulting

We offer ongoing team consulting with our Geoteaming Team Works system. Designed to assess and measure improvement, this program uses cutting-edge tools to help you create a team culture and produce team results.

Keynotes

Bring John or one of our amazing facilitators to your next training session, breakout, or keynote, and we'll turn this time into an interactive team-building experience. Available for travel around the world, we'll work with you to customize your program and bring a unique experience to bring your program to life. From the 7 Keys to Cross Team Collaboration to OpTEAMize, Maximizing Your Team Resources to Digital Team Building, look to bring cutting-edge and effective team building to your next meeting.

Contact us at http://geoteaming.com and click Request a Quote to speak to one of our Account Executives today!

Be Published in John Chen's Next Book

Share your digital team-building game with other readers!

- Do you have a digital team-building game that makes your team highly effective?
- Do you have a digital team-building game that shows teams how to use a digital tool?
- Do you have a digital team-building game that everybody raves about?

- Have you learned a team lesson that you live by through a digital team-building game?
- Do you see many teams making the same mistake during a digital team-building game?
- What team-building idea are you really passionate about?

Submitting your digital team-building game to be published is easy!

The format is the same as *50 Digital Team-Building Games*. Just go to http://50digital teambuildinggames.com and complete the submission form.

If your digital team-building game is approved, your name and biographical information will appear with the digital team-building game in the book!

Join the ranks of other highly successful executives, trainers, managers, and facilitators who have already submitted their digital team-building games.

Don't delay—the publishing deadline is coming fast.

INDEX